# Scotscape

## LORE, LEGEND AND CUSTOMS

*Edited by*
IAN D. HENDRY

GRAHAM STEPHEN

# OLIVER & BOYD

The name *Scotscape* is intended to imply that we have tried to present a broad approach to our subject, rather than explore particular aspects in detail. It is our intention in *Scotscape*, to provide samples from the great variety of song, poem, story and custom, which we as a nation have inherited as part of our culture.

As we approach the twenty-first century, many of our old customs and patterns of speech appear to be in danger of dying out. We hope that your interest and affection for this native Scots may keep them alive.

I.D.H.

G.S.

The publisher gratefully acknowledges the financial assistance of the Scottish Arts Council in the publication of this volume.

*Illustrations by David Brogan and maps by John Dugan.*

COVER PHOTOGRAPHS
*Black Rock Cottage, Buchaille Etive Mohr, Glencoe* (Roberto Matassa);
*Burryman, South Queensferry* (Lothian Studio);
*Tossing the Caber, Border Riding, Seals* (Scottish Tourist Board).

Oliver & Boyd
Croythorn House
23 Ravelston Terrace
Edinburgh EH4 3TJ

*A Division of Longman Group Ltd*

ISBN 0 05 003011 6

Printed in Great Britain by
T. & A. Constable Ltd., Edinburgh

# Contents

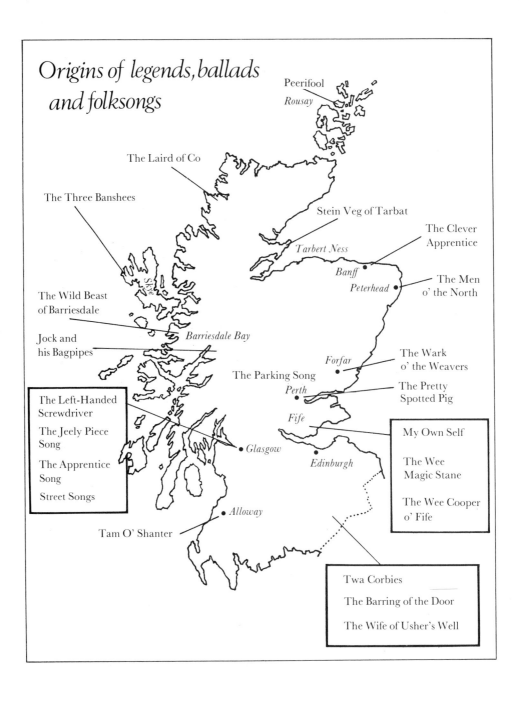

# Origins of legends, ballads and folksongs

Peerifool
*Rousay*

The Laird of Co

The Three Banshees

Stein Veg of Tarbat

The Clever Apprentice

*Tarbert Ness*

*Banff*

*Peterhead*

The Men o' the North

The Wild Beast of Barriesdale

*Skye*

Jock and his Bagpipes

*Barriesdale Bay*

The Parking Song

*Forfar*

The Wark o' the Weavers

*Perth*

The Pretty Spotted Pig

*Fife*

The Left-Handed Screwdriver

The Jeely Piece Song

The Apprentice Song

Street Songs

*Glasgow*

*Edinburgh*

My Own Self

The Wee Magic Stane

The Wee Cooper o' Fife

*Alloway*

Tam O' Shanter

Twa Corbies

The Barring of the Door

The Wife of Usher's Well

# Festivals and Customs

## HALLOWE'EN

From ghoulies and ghosties and long-legged beasties
And things that go bump in the night,
Good Lord deliver us.

Hallowe'en was the night when anything could happen. Strange creatures might prowl the streets and the countryside, witches fly on broomsticks in the sky, ghosts could knock on doors pretending to be friends of the family who would let them in. It was the night when wells might run dry, animals safely shut up in stables and byres get loose – a night of mysterious spells and magic. These were the beliefs that led to the practice of certain customs on All Hallows Eve – October 31st, the day before the start of winter.

People put willow twigs in front of their doors and windows to keep evil spirits away, and made sure they kept their fires burning to prevent strange creatures coming down the chimney. They might also put a cheese on the doorstep to feed any passing witch in the hope that she would not bother them. Big bonfires were lit on hills near towns and villages, and afterwards a large circle would be made with the ashes and everyone would put a stone inside the circle. (The next day the people would go to see whether their stones were still in the same place – if any had been moved it was a sign from evil spirits that the person whose stone it was would die within the year.)

Back home after placing their stones inside the circle of ashes, feeling safe behind the willow twigs at door and windows, people might want to see what the future held for them. For instance, a girl might peel an apple, making sure the skin did not break. She would then throw the skin over her shoulder on to the floor. The way it fell would probably look like a letter of the alphabet – that would be the initial of the man she was going to marry.

> Min' hoo we dooked for aipples then?
> The traikle scones, an' ging'bread men?
> An' chestnuts roastin' in the grate
> By jumpin' oot wad tell's oor fate?

Another ploy with apples was 'dooking'. A big tub was placed on the floor and filled with water. Apples floated on the surface. If you could get hold of an apple with your teeth, and without using your hands, you would have good luck during the coming year. There are variations on 'dooking for apples'. Sometimes you hold a fork between your teeth and try to spear a floating apple, or the apple may be hanging from a string and you have to pull it off with your teeth (again, no hands).

Instead of apples, some people dangle scones covered with treacle on a string, or put them on a plate, and again you have to eat one without using your hands. It can be very messy!

People are not scared of Hallowe'en now; it is usually an excuse for a party. Decorations of broomsticks, witches, black cats, owls, bats and creatures of the night may be put up on the walls, and fierce-faced lanterns made from hollowed-out turnips.

In many parts of Scotland, it is the time for 'guising', when children dress up and wear masks and go from house to house entertaining people. Perhaps they sing one of these songs on their way:

> Tell a story,
> Sing a sang,
> Dae a dance
> Or oot ye gang!

This is the nicht
O' Hallowe'en
When a' the witches
Will be seen:

Some o' them red
And some o' them green
And some o' them like
A turkey been!

Nowadays guising is usually confined to Hallowe'en and perhaps Christmas, but many years ago, Hallowe'en was the start of a guising season that went on until Hogmanay, the last night of the year.

## HOGMANAY

Hogmanay is a great time for visiting people in their homes. It used to start with guisers calling on nearby houses. They might perform an old play known throughout Scotland in one form or another in return for rewards of sweets, cakes, oranges or pennies. Two of the characters in this play were Sir William Wallace who 'shed his blood for Scotland's rights' and 'Guid auld Dr. Broon' who said that his travels had made him 'the best auld doctor in the toon'. Other guisers might sing a Hogmanay song including the lines:

Up sticks! Doon stools!
Dinna think that we are fools!

or:

Oor feet's cauld, oor skin's thin
So gie's a piece an' let's in.
Will ye no gie us a bawbee
To see the guid new year in?

Long ago the guising children usually managed to bring home quite a lot in the way of eatables, and would carry sacks to put everything in.

> A Guid New Year to ane an' a'
> An' mony may ye see.

When factories had hooters for starting and ending shifts, they were always blown at midnight on December 31st to handsel the New Year. In many parts of the country ships' sirens, lighthouse foghorns and church bells still sound out to welcome the New Year. In their houses people drink a toast to it and then some may go out first footing. If a dark man is the first to visit you in the New Year (or first foot you) it is said to be a sign of good luck. A first footer usually brings gifts which signify Plenty – a lump of coal (or peat), a bottle of whisky or shortbread. In a coastal fishing area he might bring kippers or other smoked fish. At each house the first footer will be welcomed with a drink and perhaps a piece of black bun (a kind of cake which is practically solid dried fruit with a pastry crust) or shortbread.

In large towns, instead of visiting each other in their homes, people might gather round some central point, such as the Tron Church in Edinburgh, for a communal welcome to the New Year.

This celebration is said to be very old: it goes back to the days when men worshipped the sun and earth, and marked the point when the sun rose again after the shortest day and people could look forward to a new beginning – or, nowadays, to Burns Night.

## BURNS NIGHT

Compared to Hogmanay, Burns Night is a modern festival. People throughout Scotland and also Scots living outside Scotland, celebrate the birthday of Robert Burns on January 25th. You can find out more about Robert Burns and his poetry on pages 16–18.

Burns Suppers were originally all-male affairs, after the custom of a club founded by Burns himself, the Tarbolton Bachelors. The chief dish of the meal is haggis, with tatties (potatoes) and neeps (mashed turnip). This is brought in, all hot and steamy, with great pomp and ceremony – it is 'piped in' by a man playing a stirring march on the bagpipes and walking in front of the person carrying the haggis itself.

Before it is cut, a special guest stands up and 'addresses the haggis', and must include in his speech part of Robert Burns' eight-verse poem 'To a Haggis'. Here are three of the verses:

Fair fa' your honest, sonsie face,
Great chieftain o' the puddin'-race!
Aboon them a' ye tak your place,
    Painch, tripe, or thairm:
Weel are ye wordy of a grace
    As lang's my arm.

The groaning trencher there ye fill,
Your hurdies like a distant hill,
Your pin wad help to mend a mill
    In time o' need,
While thro' your pores the dews distil
    Like amber bead.

Ye Pow'rs wha mak mankind your care,
And dish them out their bill o' fare,
Auld Scotland wants nae skinking ware
    That jaups in luggies:
But, if ye wish her gratefu' pray'r,
    Gie her a Haggis!

During the course of the evening many speeches are made and toasts drunk, including 'To the Immortal Memory' and 'To the lassies'.

# UP-HELLY-AA

This is another festival which takes place in January, on the last Tuesday of the month. It is held only in the Shetlands, and the really big celebration is in Lerwick. Here, there is a big torchlight procession which ends up with the ceremonial burning of a Viking longship or galley which has been specially built for the occasion. The festival commemorates the part Vikings played in Shetland history, and although the only ones who dress up as Viking warriors are the 700–800 men taking part, lcd by the Guizer Jarl and his squad of 20–25 men, everybody turns out to watch.

## TOWN FESTIVALS

Have you ever taken part in a procession?

In the summer, many small towns have a celebration when people dress up as all sorts of weird and wonderful beings, and go in procession through the town, either as part of a scene on the back of a lorry, in decorated cars, on tractors, bicycles, horses, in prams or on their own two feet. Often these processions end up in the local park, where the fancy dress costumes are judged, either by a local person of importance or a personality from TV or films imported for the occasion. Perhaps there are sports and sideshows as well.

## *Miners' Galas*

In mining towns these festivals are often called Miners' Galas. One is still held each year in Edinburgh and ends up in the Queen's Park beside Holyrood Palace. But perhaps the most widely known of these town festivals are the Common Ridings, which take place through the summer in Border towns.

## *Common Ridings*

The Border towns are all quite small and though many of the people born there leave and settle far afield (and that includes Edinburgh) they like to return at the time of their home town's Common Riding.

This may be one day or several days when people from the town ride round the boundaries of the common land owned by the town. They usually elect a young man (or a man and woman) to lead them, and each town has a different name for the leader. Here are some of them:

> Galashiels has the Braw Lad
> Kelso has the Laddie
> Jedburgh has the Jeddart Callant
> Selkirk has the Cornet
> Duns has the Reiver

Sometimes the young man rides round by himself, sometimes he leads a band of people made up of everyone who can get hold of a horse or pony and is capable of riding the 20 km or so involved.

Because so many former inhabitants return, Common Ridings have become quite a tourist attraction. The leaders of several towns' Common Ridings may join in each other's celebrations, and as no two towns ever hold their Common Riding in the same week, you could go to all of them if you wished!

## COUNTRY FESTIVALS

### *Highland Games*

In the Highlands, a time when people traditionally take a holiday in the summer is the day of their local Highland Games. Perhaps you have heard of some of the competitions that take place, such as tossing the caber (the trunk of a fir tree about 6 m long and 55–60 kg in weight), putting the shot and throwing the wooden-shafted hammer. You have probably seen variations of the last two if you have been to an athletics meeting or watched one on television. Very often children take part in Highland Dancing competitions, and Piping contests are also held.

People sometimes have to travel quite a distance to their local Highland Games, which are usually held in an ordinary field which has been emptied of cattle or sheep for the occasion.

The highlight of the games year is the world famous Braemar Gathering held every September. The Braemar Gathering has been patronised by members of the Royal Family back to the reign of Queen Victoria.

## CULTURAL FESTIVALS

Nowadays, the word 'Festival' usually makes people think of a special week or weeks during which exhibitions are held and special performances of plays and concerts are given. Most areas have Community Drama Festivals, when amateur dramatic companies compete for a prize. Some areas, such as Craigmillar in Edinburgh, have their own special week when all sorts of happenings are arranged. One of the newest is the Festival of Youth Orchestras in Aberdeen, when groups of young musicians from all over the world gather for about ten days of music making. But perhaps the best known throughout the world is the Edinburgh Festival, which was started in 1947.

For three weeks each year, there are special art exhibitions and world-famous theatre, opera and ballet companies, orchestras and soloists perform to an international audience. That is the official Edinburgh Festival. There is also the unofficial side, known as The Fringe, largely made up of small amateur companies, mostly university students, who put on shows, often written by themselves, in all sorts of small halls dotted throughout the city. Lastly, there is the biggest tourist attraction of all, The Military Tattoo, which is held on the Esplanade of Edinburgh Castle. This is an occasion for the men from the Armed Services and some of the public services, such as the Fire Service, to show what they can do. Usually there are also some guest performers from other lands, such as the dancers who came one year from Sri Lanka and had a baby elephant in their show. Often some of the items are very exciting. The Tattoo always ends with the lone piper who is picked out in the dark by spotlights as he plays a lament high up on the castle ramparts. It is a very dramatic ending to a colourful show.

# *Mixter-Maxter*

For a small country with a small population, Scotland has produced quite a number of poets of stature, both in the past and present. Despite the supposed 'dourness' of the Scot, perhaps because of it, the Scottish poet seems able to express his thoughts easily, and in warm and simple terms.

Mixter-Maxter is a collection of Scottish poetry old and new.

## HUGH MACDIARMID

*Hugh MacDiarmid* Born Langholm, educated Langholm Academy. Senior journalist, *Montrose Review*, socialist town councillor and JP in Montrose. Served in RAMC in First World War until invalided out after Salonika. Returned to journalism, concentrating mainly on literary reviews. Emergence as poet. Much of early work in Scots. Revival of writing in Scots in twentieth century largely due to his efforts. Later change to use of English considered to mark end of his best poetry. Involved in both nationalist and communist politics. Hon. LL.D., Edinburgh 1967. *Collected Poems* 1962, *Selected Poems* 1970, *Anthology* 1972.

## The Little White Rose

The Rose of all the world is not for me,
I want for my part
Only the little white rose of Scotland
That smells sharp and sweet – and breaks the heart.

Hugh MacDiarmid.

## The Bubblyjock

It's hauf like a bird and hauf like a bogle,
And juist stands in the sun there and bouks.
It's a wunder its heid disna burst
The way it's aye raxin' its chouks.

Syne it twists its neck like a serpent
But canna get oot a richt note
For the bubblyjock swallowed the bagpipes
And the blether stuck in its throat.

Hugh MacDiarmid

# NORMAN MACCAIG

*Norman MacCaig* Born in Edinburgh and educated Edinburgh University (classics). Reader in English, Stirling University. Keen observer of people and landscapes. Publications include *Far Cry*, 1943; *The Inward Eye*, 1946; *Riding Lights*, 1955; *The Sinai Sort*, 1957; *Measures*, 1965; *Rings on a Tree*, 1968; *The White Bird*, 1973.

## *Interruption to a Journey*

The hare we had run over
Bounced about the road
On the springing curve
Of its spine.

Cornfields breathed in the darkness.
We were going through the darkness and
The breathing cornfields from one
Important place to another.

We broke the hare's neck
And made that place, for a moment,
The most important place there was,
Where a bowstring was cut
And a bow was broken for ever
That had shot itself through so many
Darknesses and cornfields.

It was left in that landscape.
It left us in another.

Norman MacCaig

*Alexander Laing*  Born Brechin 1787. Second son of ploughman. Taught to read by his mother and attended school for only two winters. During his first job as a 'herd', he collected ballads and songs in broadsheet. At 16 he started apprenticeship as 'heckler' during which he composed many songs. His first poem – a love song – appeared in *Montrose Review*. Contributed to various local newspapers and magazines throughout his life. Last occupation, packman, enabled him to enjoy long daily walks through the countryside. Best known collection of poems, *Wayside Flowers*, first published 1846 and recently reissued.

## The Mowdiwort

O Mowdie! Mowdie! come ye agen,
There's tow i' ye're rock, an' ye maun spin;
For, gin we speak o' thrift to you,
We'll get nae mair o' ye're fash e'enow.

Sae play ye're pranks i' the barley craft,
An' corn-rig, whare the yird is saft,
Or try ye're pith, an' sharp ye're taes,
I' the stanie bawks, an' whinnie braes.

An' whan John Frost agen grips hard,
Ye may tak the beild o' our kailyard –
Till kindly Spring thow bank an' brake;
Till ye hear the dinnle o' spade an' rake.

Our cabbage an' greens maun grow for you,
Our sybows an' leeks that season our broo,
Till Simmer is ower maun a' be spar'd,
If ye wad *Winter* in our kailyeard.

Alexander Laing.

*Mowdiwort* is an old Scots term for a mole.

In the county of Angus, there used to be an old superstition about how to get rid of moles in a garden. First one had to collect sprigs of broom, wind pieces of flax round the tip of each sprig, and then stick a sprig of broom into each molehill, reciting the following lines three times for each mole-hill:

O Mowdie! Mowdie! come ye agen,
There's tow i' ye're rock, an' ye maun spin.

Alexander Laing learned of this charm from an old woman whom he saw mole-scaring in the Spring of 1815.

## J. K. ANNAND

*J. K. Annand* Born Edinburgh, educated Broughton Secondary School and Edinburgh University. Teacher, except for six years at sea in World War Two. At school developed interest in poetry and Lowland Scots Language, building on native Edinburgh tongue by contact with Lothian shepherds, Lanarkshire miners and Nithsdale farm folk as well as by reading other writers in Scots. Edited Braid Scots number of school magazine and since then *Lines Review* in 1958 and 1959; editor of *Lallans* since its foundation in 1973. Publications include *Sing it Aince for Pleisure*, *Twice for Joy* (both books of rhymes for children), *Two voices* and *Poems and Translations* (both poetry). Contributes essays to various periodicals. Edited, with introductory essay, *Early Lyrics by Hugh MacDiarmid*.

## The Tod

The slee tod cam to the ferm toun
Ae simmer nicht, ae simmer nicht,
And said to himself as he snowked the air,
'There's gaislins there, there's gaislins there.'

He slippit by the wee cot-hoose
Where aa slept crouse, where aa slept crouse,
He won the shed where the gaislins bide
And gaed inside, and gaed inside.

He waled oot ane o middle size,
A bonnie prize, a bonnie prize,
He grippit it ablow the heid
And kilt it deid, and kilt it deid.

He aff for hame by the muirland track,
Bird on back, bird on back,
Bringin for his bairns' delyte
A tasty bite, a tasty bite.

J. K. Annand.

## Navy

'What gart ye jine the navy, Jock?'
My faither was a sodger,
He spak eneuch o Flanders glaur
To mak me be a dodger.

I lippent on a warm dry bed,
My baccy and my rum,
A cleanly daith and a watery grave
Gif Davy Jones soud come.

I little thocht to doss me doun
In a craft sae smaa and frail
Wi hammock slung ablow the deck
That leaks like the Grey Mear's tail.

And little I thocht to be lockit in
A magazine like a jyle,
Or end my days in the chokin clart
O a sea befylt wi ile.

J. K. Annand.

## WILLIAM SOUTAR

*William Soutar* Born Perth 1898, educated Perth and Edinburgh University. In Royal Navy during World War One where contracted form of food poisoning which affected his spine and made him bed-ridden for last fourteen years of his life. Regarded as one of Scotland's finest lyric poets.

## *Supper*

Steepies for the bairnie
Sae moolie in the mou';
Parritch for a strappin lad
To mak his beard grow.

Stovies for a muckle man
To keep him stout and hale:
A noggin for the auld carl
To gar him sleep weel.

Bless the meat, and bless the drink,
And the hand that steers the pat:
And be guid to beggar-bodies
When they come to your yett.

William Soutar

Aince upon a day my mither said to me:
Dinna cleip an' dinna rype
An' dinna tell a lee.
For gin ye cleip a craw sall name ye,
An' gin ye rype a daw sall shame ye;
An' a snail sall heeze its hornies oot
An' hike them roun' an' roun' aboot
Gin ye tell a lee.

Aince upon a day, as I walkit a' my lane,
I met a daw, an' monie a craw,
An' a snail upon a stane.
Up gaed the daw an' didna shame me:
Up gaed ilk craw an' didna name me:
But the wee snail heez'd its hornies oot
An' hik'd them roun' an' roun' aboot
An' – goggl'd at me.

William Soutar.

## ROBERT BURNS

*Robert Burns*   Born 1759 in Alloway, Ayrshire. Taught to read and write by local schoolmaster, continued education at Kirkoswald. Started farming, very unsuccessfully. First wrote poems for amusement of friends and to break monotony of toil on land. On father's death took over Mossgeil farm and on failure of this decided to emigrate. In order to raise funds for this produced Kilmarnock edition of his poems in 1786, their success led him to publish them in Edinburgh and abandon idea of emigration. Returned to Ayrshire, married Jean Armour and farmed at Ellisland, Dumfriesshire. Became exciseman and gave up farming again in 1791. Died aged 37 worn out by illness, insecurity and the harsh life of farming.

Throughout his life wrote poems, songs, ballads and sonnets. His keen observation of natural surroundings and his fellow-man resulted in some of his finest poetry.

## *On Seeing a Wounded Hare Limp by Me*
### (Which a fellow had just shot at)

Inhuman man! curse on thy barb'rous art,
   And blasted be thy murder-aiming eye;
   May never pity soothe thee with a sigh,
Nor ever pleasure glad thy cruel heart!

Go, live, poor wanderer of the wood and field!
   The bitter little that of life remains:
   No more the thickening brakes and verdant plains
To thee shall home, or food, or pastime yield.

Seek, mangled wretch, some place of wonted rest,
   No more of rest, but now thy dying bed!
   The sheltering rushes whistling o'er thy head,
The cold earth with thy bloody bosom prest.

Oft as by winding Nith, I, musing, wait
   The sober eve, or hail the cheerful dawn;
   I'll miss thee sporting o'er the dewy lawn,
And curse the ruffian's aim, and mourn thy hapless fate.

Robert Burns

## From 'To a Mountain Daisy'

Wee, modest, crimson-tippèd flow'r,
Thou's met me in an evil hour;
For I maun crush amang the stoure
    Thy slender stem:
To spare thee now is past my pow'r,
    Thou bonnie gem.

Alas! it's no thy neebor sweet,
The bonnie lark, companion meet!
Bending thee 'mang the dewy weet
    Wi' spreckl'd breast,
When upward-springing, blythe to greet,
    The purpling east.

Cauld blew the bitter-biting north
Upon thy early, humble birth;
Yet cheerfully thou glinted forth
    Amid the storm,
Scarce rear'd above the parent earth
    Thy tender form.

The flaunting flow'rs our gardens yield,
High shelt'ring woods and wa's maun shield;
But thou, beneath the random bield
    O' clod or stane,
Adorns the histie stibble-field,
    Unseen, alane.

There, in thy scanty mantle clad,
Thy snawie bosom sun-ward spread,
Thou lifts thy unassuming head
    In humble guise;
But now the share uptears thy bed,
    And low thou lies!

Robert Burns

## EDWIN MORGAN

*Edwin Morgan*   Glaswegian, educated at Glasgow University where he is currently lecturer in Department of English Studies. Skilled translator of verse from Italian, French, Russian and other languages into Scots. Frequent broadcaster. Work regularly published in periodicals. Co-editor of some volumes of *Scottish Poetry*. One of the foremost Scottish poets using 'concrete poetry'.

In the Chaffinch Map of Scotland on the next page, Edwin Morgan has used the wide variety of local names for the bird to build up his outline of Scotland. Read aloud the poem also has the interesting effect of sounding like the bird in song.

# The Chaffinch Map of Scotland

```
                 chaffinch
              chaffinchaffinch
           chaffinchaffinchaffinch
           chaffinchaffinchaffinch
              chaffinchaffinch
                 chaffinch
          chaffie     chye    chaffiechaffie
          chaffie     chye    chaffiechaffie
                      chye   chaffie
               chaffiechaffiechaffie
               chaffiechaffiechaffie
                   chaffiechaffie
                   chaffiechaffie
                   chaffiechaffie
                   chaffiechaffie


                  shillyshelly
              shelfyshilfyshellyshilly
                 shelfyshillyshilly
                 shilfyshellyshelly
              shilfyshelfyshelly
                      shellyfaw
                  shielyshellyfaw

          shilfy
       shilfyshelfy shielyshiely
    shilfyshelfyshelfy        shielychaffie
       chaffiechaffie       chaffiechaffie
       chaffiechaffie
   shilfyshilfyshilfyshelfyshelfy
chaffieshilfyshilfyshelfyshelfyshelfyshelfy
chaffieshilfyshilfyshelfyshelfyshelfyshelfyshelfy
   shilfyshilfyshilfyshelfy        shelfyshelfy
  shilfy       shilfy
              shilfy
           shilfyshelfy
```

Edwin Morgan

brichtie

# The Computer's First Christmas Card

jollymerry
hollyberry
jollyberry
merryholly
happyjolly
jollyjelly
jellybelly
bellymerry
hollyheppy
jollyMolly
marryJerry
merryHarry
hoppyBarry
heppyJarry
boppyheppy
berryjorry
jorryjolly
moppyjelly
Mollymerry
Jerryjolly
bellyboppy
jorryhoppy
hollymoppy
Barrymerry
Jarryhappy
happyboppy
boppyjolly
jollymerry
merrymerry
merrymerry
merryChris
ammerryasa
Chrismerry
asMERRYCHR
YSANTHEMUM

Edwin Morgan

## GEORGE MACKAY BROWN

*George Mackay Brown* Born Orkney 1921. Educated Stromness Academy, Newbattle Abbey College and Edinburgh University. Encouraged at Newbattle by the Principal, fellow-Orcadian Edwin Muir. Except for brief absences, has lived in Orkney all his life. Literary themes mainly concerned with Orkneys and Norse forebears. Publications (poetry, short stories and plays) include *The Storm and other Poems, Loaves and Fishes, The Year of the Whale, A Spell for Green Corn, Greenvoe,* and *Magnus.*

## *Unlucky boat*

That boat has killed three people. Building her
Sib drove a nail through his thumb and died in his croft
Bunged to the eyes with rust and penicillin.
One evening when the Brine was a bar of silver
Under the moon, and Mansie and Tom with wands
Were putting a spell on cuithes, she dipped a bow
And ushered Mansie, his pipe still in his teeth,
To meet the cold green angels. They hauled her up
Among the rocks, right in the path of Angus,
Whose neck, rigid with pints from the Dounby Market,
Snapped like a barley stalk. . . . There she lies,
A leprous unlucky bitch, in the quarry of Moan.

Tinkers, going past, make the sign of the cross.

George Mackay Brown

## MARION ANGUS

*Marion Angus* 1866–1946. Born and brought up in Arbroath, a daughter of the manse. Contributed short stories and poems to various magazines and periodicals, but only began to write seriously in middle years. First collection of poems, *The Lilt and Other Verses* published 1922, followed by several others. Final volume, *Lost Country*, published 1937. The underlying current of haunting sadness running through much of her work contributes to the plaintive quality which distinguishes it in style and content from that of her contemporaries.

### The Fox's Skin

When the wark's a' dune and the world's a' still,
And whaups are swoopin' across the hill,
And mither stands cryin', 'Bairns, come ben,'
It's the time for the Hame o' the Pictish Men.

A sorrowfu' wind gaes up and doon,
An' me my lane in the licht o' the moon,
Gaitherin' a bunch o' the floorin' whin,
Wi' my auld fur collar hapt roond ma chin.

A star is shining on Morven Glen –
It shines on the Hame o' the Pictish Men.
Hither and yont their dust is gane.
But ane o' them's keekin' ahint yon stane.

His queer auld face is wrinkled and riven,
Like a raggedy leaf, sae drookit and driven.
There's nocht to be feared at his ancient ways,
For this is a' that iver he says:

'The same auld wind at its weary cry:
The blin'-faced moon in the misty sky;
A thoosand years o' clood and flame,
An' a'things the same an' aye the same –
The lass is the same in the fox's skin,
Gaitherin' the bloom o' the floorin' whin.'

Marion Angus

## STEPHEN MULRINE

*Stephen Mulrine*  Born in Glasgow in 1937. Currently a lecturer in the Glasgow School of Art. He also writes plays and scripts of various kinds for television and radio.

## *The Coming of the Wee Malkies*

Whit'll ye dae when the wee Malkies come,
if they dreep doon affy the wash-hoose dyke
an pit the hems oan the sterrheid light,
an play keepie-up oan the clean close-wa',
an blooter yir windae in wi' the ba',
missis, whit'll ye dae?

Whit'll ye dae when the wee Malkies come,
if they chap yir door an' choke yir drains,
an caw the feet fae yir sapsy weans,
an tummle thur wulkies through yir sheets,
an tim thur ashes oot in the street,
missis, whit'll ye dae?

Whit'll ye dae when the wee Malkies come,
if they chuck thur screwtaps doon the pan,
an stick the heid oan the sanit'ry man;
when ye hear thum come shauchlin doon yir loaby,
chantin', 'Wee Malkies! The gemme's . . . a bogey!'
Haw, missis, whit'll ye dae?

Stephen Mulrine

*Children in a Glasgow cinema queue* by Joan Eardley

# ALAN JACKSON

*Alan Jackson*   Born 1938. Educated at Edinburgh University. Has worked as labourer between periods of writing. Gives readings of work and has acted as his own publisher and distributor. Awarded Scottish Arts Council grant 1967.

## 'tara'

tara for now the tadpole said
and tucked his tadtail round his head
i'll sink to the bottom but i won't be dead

Alan Jackson

# Rhymes, Riddles an' Rinnin' Aboot

## NURSERY RHYMES & SONGS

Often the first thing we hear as children is a nursery rhyme. Today many of the old Scots nursery rhymes are still in use after hundreds of years.

### Alie balie

Alie balie, alie balie bee.
Sittin' on yer mammie's knee,
Greetin' for anither bawbee,
To buy some sugar candy.

### Clap, clap

Clap, clap handies
Mammie's wee, wee ain,
Clap, clap handies,
Daddie's comin' hame.
Hame till his wee, bonnie,
Wee bit laddie,
Clap, clap handies.

*Jumping Jack* by Walter Geikie

26

# RHYMES FOR FUN

Many rhymes which Scottish children used to sing and say were fun or nonsense rhymes. Some of them were parts of games, others were just good fun to say.

Adam and Eve gaed up my sleeve,
Tae fess me doon some gundy.
Adam and Eve cam doon ma sleeve,
And said there was nane till Monday.

I've a kistie,
I've a creel,
I've a baggie,
Fu' o' meal.

Sugar-ally watter;
As black as the lum;
Gether up the preens,
And ye'll a get some.

I've a doggie,
At the door,
One, two,
three, four.

* Lady, Lady Landers,
    Tak your coats aboot yer heid,
    And flee awa to Flanders.

*This rhyme used to be chanted by children when they threw ladybirds into the air.

Try to say these three Tongue-twisters as quickly as you can.

The crockit quetit cook o Coulter
Gid wi a cloutit cloak,
A cloutit clout tae clout it wi,
Tae clout the cloutit cloak.

The black-backit pairtrick,
Flew ower the Kirk o' Cortachy.

Rob Low's lum reeks,
Roond aboot the chimley cheeks
Wi' a pair o' blue breeks.

If a boy or girl was going to tell tales on the others, the following, rhyme was often chanted.

> Tell-tale tit,
> Your tongue shall be slit,
> An' a' the doggies in the street,
> Shall get a wee bit.
>
> Tell-tale tit,
> Yer Mammy cannae knit,
> Yer Daddy cannae go tae bed,
> Wi'oot a dummy tit.

Crowds of school children in Glasgow would often chant this rhyme.

> Oor wee school's the best wee school
> The best wee school in Glesca.
> A' that's wrang wi' oor wee school's
> The baldy wee heidmaister.
> He goes tae the pub on a Setterday night,
> He goes tae the Church on Sunday,
> And prays tae the Lord tae gie him strength
> Tae belt the weans on Monday.

Each generation invents its own style of fun rhymes. This one is based on a popular song some years back.

> Ye dae sixteen sums an' what dae ye get,
> Fifteen wrang and six o' the belt,
> Hey, teacher, don't ye call me
>     'cause I can't come,
> 'Cause I'm stuck tae ma seat
>     wi' bubbly gum.

This rhyme was often chanted as a part of a skipping or hopping game.

John Smith, fellow fine,
Can ye shoe a wee horse o' mine?
Yes indeed, and that I can,
Just as well as any man.
First a nail and then a prod
Now, wee man, yer horse is shod.

## Pussie at the Fireside

A rhyme chanted by children when a child has fallen or hurt himself, as a result of doing something silly.

Pussie at the fireside
 Suppin up brose,
Doon cam a cinder,
 An' burnt Pussie's nose.
'Oh! cried Pussie,
 'That's nae fair!
'Weel, said the cinder,
 'Ye sudna be there!'

31

## I ring, I ring, a Pinky

The reciter of this rhyme tells of all the terrible things which may happen to people who tell lies.

I ring, I ring, a pinky,
If I tell a lee,
I'll gang tae the bad place
Whenever I dee,
White pan, black pan,
Burn me tae death,
Tak a muckle gully,
An' cut ma breath,
Ten miles below the earth.

## Horny Golach

The horny gollach's an awesome beast,
  Souple an' scaley;
He has twa horns an' a hantle o' feet
An' a forky tailie.

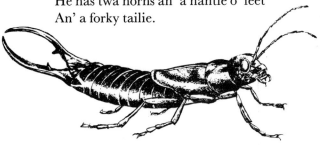

## Rattlesteens

A rhyme chanted by children when it comes on rain.

Rainy, rainy, rattlesteens,
Dinna rain on me;
Rain on John O' Groat's hoose,
Far owre the sea.

# RIDDLES

A riddle is a kind of puzzle. The reader has to try to work out what the answer is from what is written in the riddle. Here are three old Scots riddles to test the reader.

## Who am I?

Baith early and late
He chaps at the door;
And gangs on his gait
To rich and to puir.

He has a fou poke
O' gledness and pain
And wales for maist folk
What he never will ken.

## What am I?

Here is a truth ye canna dout
Sin your ain sicht may see
A body, naither bird nor brute,
That can baith roar and flee.

It soums abune the heichest clude
And owre the faem will fare;
And though it has nor banes nor bluid
Yet banes and bluid are there.

## What am I?

It comes wi' warmer weather,
But in wintry days is gaen;
It likes na to forgether
And is no often seen.

It winna big a housie
Yet its bairn has aye a hame;
And it sings awa richt crousie
Though its words are aye the same.

*Answers on page 34*

The counting out rhymes on the past few pages were only used to start off games, to decide who was to be 'it' or the 'outie'.

The games themselves were often complicated and different areas would have slightly different versions. Many games were strictly street games, but in recent years, because of the huge increase in road traffic, these games have been driven off the streets and many have disappeared. Two favourite street games of 30 years ago were:

## Red Lights

Red Lights was usually played by girls. One girl would stand with her back to the others, who stood on the other side of the street. They would have to try to cross over the street without being seen. When the 'out' girl had counted ten, she turned round, shouting 'Red Lights!' If anyone moved when she whirled round then that person had to go back to the starting place again. The winner was the first person to get past the 'out' girl and touch the wall.

## Giant Steps and Baby Steps

This was another street crossing game. The 'Outie' stood on one kerb, facing the others. He or she then told the others what kind of steps to take. These orders could include large steps like 'giant steps' or tiny steps like 'baby steps', or 'hot and cold water bottles' – running or walking, 'banana-slides' – sliding, 'scissors' – crossing legs and hopping – and many other ways of moving. The winner was the person who reached the opposite kerb first. He or she would be the next 'outie' and get to call the orders.

*Answers to Riddles*   A postman, An aeroplane, A cuckoo.

There are many little songs and chants which go with the games. Here is a selection of chants which go with skipping and ball games.

## Skipping Rhyme

Mrs Brown went to town,
Riding on a pony,
When she came back,
She lost her hat,
And called on Miss Maloney.

## Hopping or Skipping Rhyme

Ickerty-pickerty,
Pies-a-lickerty
Pumpaleerie-jig!

## Skipping Song

Cowboy Joe,
From Mexico,
Hands up, stick 'em up,
Cowboy Joe.

## Ball Game Chant

One, two, three, four,
Mary at the kitchen door,
Eating cherries off a plate
Down fell the summer seat,
I've a kistie, I've a creel,
I've a baggie fu' o' meal,
I've a doggie at the door,
One, two, three, four.

## Ball Game Chant

One, two, three a-leerie,
I see Mrs Peerie,
Sittin' on her bum-ba-leerie,
Eatin' fried tomatoes.

Certain pastimes did and still do have times of the year when they are played most.

## Conkers or chessies – September–November

Conkers are the ripe fruit of chestnuts which, when brown and hard, are bored and threaded on a string. One person tries to crack his opponent's chestnut by swinging his own 'chessie' at it. The winner is the one who cracks or breaks his opponent's.

Boys used to carry long strings of chestnuts to school, at play and almost everywhere, during the 'chessie' season.

## Boolies (marbles) – February–April

There are a great many different ways to play with boolies, ringie, kypes and many other variations. Most boolies used nowadays are made of coloured glass and have taken over from the 'piggers' and 'steelers' of former years.

'Piggers' were large rough earthenware marbles while 'steelers' were ball bearings of all sizes and coming from articles of all descriptions such as bicycle crank cases.

## Girds

One pastime which has disappeared in recent years is that of playing with a gird and a cleek. As recently as the 1950s a large number of boys and girls would have been found, in town and country, playing with girds. A gird was an iron hoop and a cleek an iron hook with which the 'girder' pushed and steered the gird. When a gird broke it was usually taken along to the local blacksmith, who very often would repair it for nothing!

One of the most exciting things about girding was the sound made by a gird as it rolled over the surface of the road or pavement. Boys, and sometimes girls, would 'gird' a long way, often spanning 10–20 kilometres between villages. The gird, like many street games, has been more or less killed off by the combined forces of the motor car and television.

## Hopscotch

A favourite girls' game is Hopscotch, or Beddies or Peevers as it is known in some areas.

Beddies is played outside on a pavement, playground or any hard flat surface. A grid shape is drawn and the players use a piece of stone or slate, called a 'peever', rather like a counter in a table game. The player slides the 'peever' on to the grid and then hops in and out of the squares of the grid.

There are many variations of this game:

A. An easy form of Beddies has a grid of four lines and five spaces, marked out one to five. The players have to hop over the lines and have to move the peever from one space to another.

B. A more difficult version of Beddies has numbers going up to nine or ten, and has a cross shape in the middle of the grid. The players put one foot into the grid and have to progress in a series of hops and jumps with feet astride for the double blocks. When they reach the top of the grid they have to jump (legs astride) and hop and jump back to the beginning.

Beddies or Hopscotch used to be a very popular game for girls, and it is still played in some parts of Scotland.


## Cattie and Battie

Another very popular game which was played by generations of children was Cattie and Battie.

This game was played with a bat and a 'cattie' – a short, thick piece of wood sharpened at both ends. The game was played rather like rounders or Glasgow Ringies, with places marked where a player could stand safely, while moving round the court towards home base. The 'cattie' was laid on the ground and the player struck one of the sharp ends sharply with the 'battie'. This caused the 'cattie' to spin up into the air, then the player struck it with the bat, threw the bat down and started to run round the ring.

## Pilers

Making and riding pilers, or bogies or cairties as they are known elsewhere, is still a popular pastime. An old set of wheels, some wood, nails and rope is all that is required to make a piler or bogie. In times before 'chopper' bikes and plastic go-carts, bogies used to be very popular and boys would spend a great deal of time painting their bogies in bright colours, giving them names and having races.

There is an exciting story about a piler race in *The Goalkeeper's Revenge and Other Stories* by Bill Naughton.

Many of these games are now dead, yet surprisingly, despite the glamour of modern toys and the lure of television, some of the old games which have been favoured by generations of Scottish children still continue to flourish. What is more important, new games and variations of old games continue to keep pace with modern life in Scotland.

# Fairs
# and Markets

Have you ever been to Aikey Fair? Perhaps you've seen the Burry Man or the Lang Toun Lass? Perhaps you haven't heard of any of these, but all over Scotland fairs and markets are held every year and people get together to sing, laugh, dance, play. . . .

In this chapter you will find out a little about fairs and markets, and some of the unusual customs that still take place in Scotland.

*Roundabout* by Walter Geikie

## Auld Aikey

How did fairs start? There are many stories, but one that is often told concerns an old pedlar called Aikey. He tramped around the country with a pack full of goods on his back. He tried to sell his goods wherever he could. One day, while he was travelling through the parish of Old Deer in Buchan he came to a stream. As he was crossing he slipped and fell in. He howled and spluttered in the cold water, but managed to struggle ashore.

'Man, I'm soaked,' Auld Aikey gasped as he lay on the bank. He took off his pack and emptied out the contents.

'Soaked tae,' he said sadly, 'I'd as weel lay them oot tae dry.'

The pedlar laid out the bright cloths and ribbons on the grass and sat down to wait for the sun to dry them. After a while some people from the nearby village came along. A woman stopped.

'That's bonny stuff you've got there, pedlar,' she said.

'Aye, and cheap too,' replied Auld Aikey. 'They're a bit weet, for I fell in the water, but they're still fine quality.'

He picked up a length of red cloth.

'Feel that for yourself,' he said. 'Is that no' fine stuff?'

'It's fine stuff indeed,' the woman answered, 'and I believe I'll buy it frae you.'

Soon the other villagers had crowded round and Auld Aikey was doing a good trade. He did so well that he promised to come back the following year. He kept his promise. Soon other pedlars heard of this market and came to lay out their goods. As the years went by the market grew and grew, but it was still called Aikey Fair in memory of the old pedlar who started it all by falling in the water.

Nobody knows if that story is true, but it might well be. Here is another piece about Aikey Fair. Buchan is in Aberdeenshire, and many people there work on farms. In this story a farmworker remembers Aikey Fair in his young days and tells how the fair started.

## At the Fair

In the old days down in the Howe o' Buchan hoeing and haymaking were always associated with Aikey Fair. If you were finished with the hyow and well forrit with the hay you had a good chance of a day off for Aikey. . . .

Aikey Fair was considered a general holiday, and apart from term and market days, and a day off at the New Year, it was about the only holiday you would get. Wednesday was the recognised day of the Fair, the first Wednesday after the nineteenth of July, but if your boss wasn't a kirk elder you could jump on your bike and take a run up on the Sunday before then, when the fun really started. If you didn't care a damn you went in any case, but sometimes it was frowned upon in those days.

Aikey used to be a horse fair, when all the lads would be there with their horses for the market, their manes rolled and their tails tied up with coloured segs, standing in two rows like patient cavalry, waiting a buyer. . . .

And you told the quine about the Holy Fair that the monks had started for the relief of the poor and the upkeep of their abbey at Auld Deer. This Holy Day became a local holiday and was the beginning of the fair, but it was named after a tink who fell in the Ugie burn with his pack and got soaked and spread his trinkets out to dry on the Brae. And the folks on their way to Auld Deer bought all the trock that Aikey had spread out in the blink of the sun. So old Aikey came back again next year on the same day with a huge pack on his back, almost all that he could stagger with, and he spread it out on the heather and the passers-by bought every knick-knack that he had. Then the old fool went away and got drunk and told all the other hawkers about the folk at Auld Deer . . . so the next year a great birn of tinks came to Aikey's Brae and some of them sold their shelts to the farming chiels and that was the start of the horse-market. Syne the gypsies came with their caravans and fortune-tellers and clowns and before long you had a real jamboree on the hillside.

You wasn't sure how it got started on a Sunday, but maybe it was because the tinks came at the weekend to get their stalls up for the Wednesday, and when there were so many ill-mannered creatures standing about watching they might as well do something, so they got yoked on the Sunday.

(From *Hard Shining Corn* by David Toulmin)

## The Feein' Markets

David Toulmin, who wrote that piece about Aikey Fair, is a farm-worker, and probably knows about the Feein' Markets, which were held twice a year. These were markets at which farm-workers were hired for the year. In May it was usually the married men who turned up, and in November, at Martinmas, it was the turn of the single men and 'loons'.

The markets were busy occasions. The men who wanted to be hired would stand about in groups, waiting for the farmers. The farmers would come and offer terms – how much they would pay, and what the workers would have to do. Often the men wore or carried something, to show what they did. A shepherd might have a bit of wool, or a dairy-man might have a bit of straw. If a man was hired, the farmer gave him a 'fee' to seal the bargain. About fifty years ago, when these markets were still being held, the fee was about a shilling, or 5p. If a man who had been hired and paid his fee broke his promise to work for the farmer he could be fined. He might have to pay twenty times the fee. That could be £1, which was a lot of money in those days. At that time, a 'loon' would get about £6.50 – not for a day's work but for six months' work! Of course, the farm-workers were allowed a certain amount of potatoes, milk, oatmeal and so on, and many lived in bothies – small cottages near the farm – without paying rent.

Feein' Markets were held all over Scotland at one time. Many people have relations such as grandmothers or grandfathers who will remember 'gettin' fee'd'.

## Aulton Market

The last time I saw the Aulton Market there were no more than a dozen horses on the field, and no gingerbread and no whisky tents. How different thirty, forty years ago. Maybe five hundred, maybe a thousand horses changed hands that day. The whisky tents seethed with roaring drunken crowds. Great piles of gingerbread and chipped apples (a handful for a penny) melted off the stalls like snow wreaths in thaw – roistering farmers staked their shillings in hopeless attempts to find the lady or spot the pea; fiddlers played reels, pipers piped laments, boxers took on all comers for a guinea, and ballad singers made the afternoon hideous with the songs of Scotland. As the evening came on, gas flares lit up the lanes between the booths, making the shadows yet more drunken as the wind troubled the flames. The town people now came in for their evening's fun – engineers from the shipyards, papermakers up from the Don and hundreds of redoubtable ladies from the Broadford mill.

(From *Farmer's Boy* by J. R. Allan)


## The Magic Cheese

Nowadays, at most fairs, there are dodgem cars, waltzers, shooting galleries, merry-go-rounds and even ghost trains. Often you will also find fortune-tellers, old women who claim to be able to read the future in the palm of your hand, or can gaze into a crystal ball and tell what is going to happen. In the past there were no dodgem cars, waltzers or the like, but there were fortune-tellers and even travelling magicians. There is an old story about a magician who appeared at Tarland Fair which, like Aikey Fair, is in Aberdeenshire. Perhaps a fortune-teller told the people at the fair that the magician would come to help them, or perhaps she knew the magician and told him of the people's troubles. Who knows? Perhaps the story isn't true – but it's worth telling.

The people of Tarland were angry. For a long time things had been stolen, and the villagers knew who was to blame – it was the tinkers who lived nearby. But the tinkers were cunning and were never caught. Besides, there were so many of them that the villagers were afraid to chase them away. The tinkers were big and strong and were scared of nothing. Even the young men of Tarland couldn't chase the tinkers away. The young men muttered a great many threats and claimed they were not afraid of the tinkers, but still they would not tackle them.

Now every year in Tarland a fair was held, and people came from all around, bringing goods to sell. As the day of the fair came closer, the people of Tarland grew more and more worried. The tinkers might frighten many people away, or might swoop down and steal whatever they could carry. On the day of the fair, however, a wizard appeared. At the same time, the tinkers came marching down the street. They were big men who shouted and bawled, and the villagers feared the worst. The fair would be ruined. It might never be held again. What could they do?

The tinkers marched on. Suddenly they stopped. In front of them they saw a little man with a big cheese. The tinkers burst out laughing. The cheese was so big, and the man so little. . . . They did not know the little man was a wizard. When he set down the cheese and knelt before it, the tinkers thought that he was terrified. They howled with laughter, they bent double with laughter. They slapped each other on the back, they pointed at the wizard. 'Look,' they cried, 'look,' but they could say no more for laughing. The wizard stood up. He took out a knife and began to cut open the cheese. Deeper and deeper he cut and the tinkers, who had now stopped laughing, watched and puzzled. Then came a terrible sound, a sound like a thousand saws cutting into wood. Louder and louder grew the noise, and the tinkers were becoming a little frightened. They looked at each other, as if to ask, 'What is it?' as if to say, 'What is making that noise, that noise like a thousand saws cutting into wood?' And then they knew, for out of the cheese poured thousands and thousands of angry bees! Instantly the tinkers turned and ran and the bees chased after them.

The people of Tarland cheered the wizard all through the village. The tinkers were never seen again. The Tarland Fair was saved.

## Street Names and Signs

Is there a Market Street where you live? Or a Market Place, or a Market Square? In most old towns you will find these names, because at one time almost every town held a market. Once, these markets were very important because they were the only means people had of buying many goods. In those days there were no cars, railways or aeroplanes, and the roads were very bad, so that things could not be carried very far, especially food.

On Market Day, the people from the countryside around the town would bring in goods to sell. They would set up stalls, and fill them with articles such as fruit, vegetables, eggs, cheese and butter. The country folk would also buy things they needed in town. There were tailors, blacksmiths, leather-workers and many other craftsmen. Since most people in medieval times could not read, the craftsman would hang a sign outside his house or shop. A tailor might have a sign showing a pair of scissors, a carpenter might have a sign showing a saw.

Here are some signs that were used in those days. Can you tell what each sign means? (Answers on page 49.)

1.

2.

3.

4.

5.

6.

Sometimes, in towns which had harbours, ships from foreign countries would arrive with goods. There might be cork from Spain, or wine from France. Often, the streets near the harbour would have names such as Baltic Street or America Street.

You can find out many things about the town or city where you live from the names of streets.

## The Royal Charter

Long ago, before the people of a town could hold a market, they had to get permission from the King or Queen. If permission was given, the townsfolk received a Royal Charter. This was a document which laid down rules, such as on what days the market could be held, and what goods could be sold.

The people of South Queensferry were granted a Royal Charter in 1363 by King David the Second. Once, the Charter was read out before the start of the market. Anyone could sell anything on a stall, as long as they paid 'the toll' – money for the right to set up a stall.

The Charter also banned all beggars from the town on the day of the market. Any beggars in the town on that day could be put in jail. In those days, too, people were put to death for many things, even for stealing a loaf of bread or a sheep, but the Charter banned all executions while the market was taking place.

## The Burry Man

South Queensferry was allowed to hold a Fair as well as a market. It was called the Ferry Fair. Markets might be held every week, but fairs took place only once a year, and in July when the time for the Ferry Fair came round you could also expect to see the Burry Man making his rounds.

He was a strange figure. In each hand he carried a long stick with flowers twined round it. Flowers also made up his headdress, hiding his face, and he wore a tight-fitting suit, covered with thistles and teazle burrs. He walked silently round the town, speaking to no one, although many people crowded behind him. From time to time he would stop at a house where he would be given a gift or money.

No one quite knows how or why the custom of the Burry Man's rounds started, but it is at least six hundred years old. Some people think he was meant to be able to carry away all the evil spirits that might be lingering in the town. But others think that, since he went round South Queensferry the day before Ferry Fair, it is more likely that he was a toll collector who collected money from those who brought goods into the town to sell from stalls at the Ferry Fair.

## A Letter from Jean

The Croft House,
Irvine,
Ayrshire.

Dear François,

When I last wrote to you I said I would tell you about the fair we
have in Irvine every year. It is called the Marymass Fair, and
people say it first started in the twelfth century. We have races
during the fair, and it is said that these races were first held over a
thousand years ago! It is said they are the oldest races in Europe.
Do you have anything like that in Paris?

I think I told you that Irvine is a very old town. It stands on the
Firth of Clyde. There is a beautiful beach with miles of golden
sand, and you can see the mountains of Arran in the distance. It's
lovely. I hope you can visit us one day and see for yourself. Perhaps
you would even come to the Marymass Fair.

We have a pageant or parade of people dressed up in historical
costumes at the fair. The two most important people in the
pageant are the Captain of the Carters' Society and the Marymass
Queen. Mary Queen of Scots used to live in France, but when she
returned to Scotland she came to Irvine. That was in 1563. Irvine
at that time was Glasgow's port. She was escorted to the Seagate
Castle by the Society of Cadgers. They were later called Carters.
In those days many things were carried from place to place by
horse, so carriers were important people. In the pageant the
Marymass Queen is always dressed like Mary Queen of Scots.

On the Sunday the week before the fair the new Captain of the
Carters is chosen. During the rest of the week there are events such
as football matches and firework displays.

The Fair is always held on the third or fourth Saturday in August,
and at ten o'clock on the morning of the Fair all the members of
the Carters' Society gather at the house of the man who was
Captain the year before. Then the new Captain marches off
around the town. A band goes in front of him and there is a long

48

procession of Carters on horses and many other people behind him. The procession goes all around the town and at noon they arrive at the Town House in the High Street. There is a platform with a throne on it. The Marymass Queen arrives in a carriage. She has four ladies-in-waiting, because Queen Mary had four ladies-in-waiting, who were all called Mary too. After the Queen is crowned the crowd sings 'Scots Wha Hae', which is a song by Robert Burns, our great poet.

Then there is a procession to the Town Moor. This was a gift to Irvine a long time ago. It was to thank the people of the town for fighting at Bannockburn. This battle, in 1314, is remembered by all Scots. King Robert the Bruce led a small army of Scots against a huge army of English led by King Edward II. The English were defeated at Bannockburn and Scotland became independent again after years of English rule.

All afternoon the famous Irvine Races are held. There are races for cart-horses, for ponies, for children and for old folk. At the end of the races the procession marches back to the Seagate Castle. Three cheers are given for the Queen and then 'Auld Lang Syne' is sung. You will probably know that song. It is known all over the world. It, too, was written by Robert Burns.

We have lots of other things during the week. There are shows, and you can buy candy floss and toffee apples and go for a ride on the Big Dipper. It's great fun. I wish you could see it. Perhaps one day you will. I hope this letter will not be too hard for you to understand.

Your Pen Pal,
Jean

*Old Shop Signs* (page 46)
1. Barber
2. Pawnbroker
3. Tobacconist
4. Nautical Instrument Maker
5. Gold-beater. (He beat gold ingots into gold leaf.)
6. Chemist

## The Lang Toun

Kirkaldy is often called the 'Làng Toun' because its main street was once six kilometres long! The town is in Fife and every year it holds the Links Market, which claims to be the largest event of its kind in the world. The Fair is very, very old, and its charter can be traced back to 1305. It begins in the middle of April and lasts a week. It is held on the Esplanade, or Links, which runs parallel to part of the High Street. For the whole week of the fair no cars are allowed on the Esplanade, only the vehicles of the travelling showmen who arrive in hundreds. They come from all over Britain. There are countless stalls, shows and machines; there are even a couple of circuses. Both sides of the Esplanade are lined for over 2 kilometres. The Esplanade, which is over 10 metres wide, is the broadest in Britàin.

There are thousands of coloured lights, which make a beautiful display, and of course, there is music and laughter. Visitors throng the fairground, but some old customs still survive. Boys can still buy pink sugar-hearts to give to their girlfriends!

Another celebration is held in Kirkcaldy at the end of June. This is the Youth Pageant Week when there are parades in fancy-dress and many kinds of entertainment. There is also a competition to choose a boy and a girl, the king and queen of the fair, who are known as the Lang Toun Lass and The Lang Toun Lad.

Many other towns have celebrations each year, when they, too, choose boys and girls to lead the festivities.

# *Young Scots Write*

Many Scottish children find great enjoyment in writing poems and stories in Scots or their local dialects.

Young Scots Write is a complete section of such pieces, written by children from all over Scotland, both in English and Scots.

## *Ma Wee Bairn*

Yer laughin' an' greetin', wakened and sleepin',
Chasin' the birdies awa,
Shoutin' and screamin', quiet an' dreamin',
But I still like ye best ava',
Yer knees are a' scurled, yer hans are pitch black,
Ye shouldna' go play in the byre,
The coos'll get freicht an' their meat winna' tak',
But ach, ye niver tire,
Ye're keekin' an' harkin' to see fit ye're missin',
Yer lessons ye jist winna' learn,
I scold ye for mischief, but you niver listen,
Ye're just ma wee bairn.

Shirley (age 14)

## My Wish

It's a dog I'd sair like,
Ane that's spotted, black 'n white,
Or, maybe ane that's black 'n broon,
Wi' bonny lugs hingin' doon,
Wi' twa bra' meltin' een,
An' a black weet nose in atween.

Bite! My dog wid never,
My dog wid be far ower clever,
I think my dog's name wid be Roy,
But only if it is a boy.
It's nae guid wishin' nicht an' day,
I should buy a dog straight away,
The thing that's stoppin' me is – payin',
So I just hiv tae go on prayin'.

Kathleen (age 10)

## Lochs

In the heart of a valley
A long elegant mirror lies
A ripple breaks upon the loch
An otter surfaces with a fish
And swims out to its holt
A lone fisherman sits on the bank.

Blair (age 12)

## Burial Procession

One day when the village
of Skara Brae was very quiet,
suddenly a scream came from
the chieftain's house and the
chieftain's wife came running
out shouting. 'He's dead,
he's dead.' Everybody knew how
the chieftain had died. He had
stuck a flint knife in his neck.

The burial procession was
set straight away to Maeshowe.
They carried the body on a stone
slab till they got to Maeshowe.
They crossed the forty-five
foot ditch and walked into
Maeshowe. They put the chieftain
in the chamber and took the other
man's skull very carefully out
of the chamber.

The sight of the chieftain
being put into the chamber and
stone slab being put into place
was too much for the chieftain's
wife, so she went berserk. One
man broke the clay pot so that
the chieftain's spirit could
go to the gods. We had a great
big feast after the ceremony.

Shaun (age 9)

## Efter a fitba match

It was a braw match, aye. The ither side played like a bunch o' auld weemin. Oor side played grand tho', aye, they did that. Did ye see Broon's fleein' heeder – richt in the corner o' the net.

I liked Stanton's goal, a richt daisy-cutter, it wis through the goalie's legs – left him standin'. That man in the ither team – canna mind his name – daen grand and Stanton stuck oot his fit and the ba' went fleein'. Aye, it was a braw match.

Alan (age 11)

## Protest

One day I sat and stared at space
And saw three men
And the expression on their face.
The one had stars and stripes
Painted on his chest.
The Second a red flag
Pinned tightly to his breast.
The Third was black
And cried for food –
The other two ignored him.
– Mission looking good –

Diann (aged 15

## Ambition

When I leave school,
I'll get a job –
Teacher,
Clerk,
Preacher,
Spark.

But now I'm just a paper boy,
On one twenty-five a week
Saving my money to buy a surprise,
A mechanical mouse that goes 'squeak', 'squeak'.

I'd like to be so big, brave and bold.
Too bad at the moment, I'm only ten years old.

Joe (age 14)

## To an Arbroath Smokie

Fair fa' when ye're upon a dish,
Ye are the king o' a' the fish,
Ye stand oot among them a',
Sole, crab or eel.
Aye, the greatest o' them a',
Ye mak' a tasty meal.

This eastern stuff like curry an' rice
Ach well, they dinna taste sae nice.
Ye are known Scotland wide,
And a' yer fame
Wid mak' paella and the likes
A' tak' shame.

Ah, yer slender and braw taste,
Wad mak' yer fishy friends tak' haste,
An' Rabbie Burns,
Wha's he kiddin'?
Ye'r better than his mealy puddin'.

Nae mair ye'll swim aboot the sea,
But mak' a meal for the likes o' me.
When are ye better
Than nature state?
On the table, in a plate.

Hamish (age 11)


## Ah've got this an' Ah've got that

Ah've got a budgie,
Ah've got a cat,
Ah've got a haggis,
Noo, what dae ye think o' that?

Ah've got a moose,
Ah've got a rat,
Ah've got a braw big hoose,
Noo, what dae ye think o' that?

Ah've got a dress,
Ah've got a hat,
Ah've got a muckle bike,
Noo, what dae ye think o' that?

Ah've got a ball,
Ah've got a bat,
Ah've got a muckle cuddy,
Noo, what dae ye think o' that?

Lucy (age 10)

## The Old Man of Hoy

(Here is a legend Peter made up about the Old Man of Hoy.)

Many thousands of years ago when Orkney was inhabited by trolls and Geerongs, there was a king called Agor. He ruled his people well and was kind to the Unicorns and Giffrafs. When he died there was no king to take his place, for he had no son. Deerin, the wise old magician, called a contest of strength to choose the new king. Floonf, Lord of the trolls, and Ploonf, his cousin, Lord of the Geerongs, came. Swift, the chief of the unicorns, and Aug, leader of the Giffrafs, and many more knights and creatures of all shapes and sizes came to try and become king.

Deerin told them they had to throw a huge rock across a loch. They all tried but none could do it. Then a great giant appeared and flung it across the loch. He was declared King and ruled for many years. When he died he was turned into stone and stands on Hoy, and when Orkney is in great danger he will wake and defeat our foes.

Peter (age 10)

*The Old Man of Hoy*

## Growing Up

As I was walking down the street,
I used to give myself a treat,
I used to buy a shillnie cake,
The kind my baker used to make.

But now I am a happy bloke,
As half my money goes up in smoke
And as I buy the great Woodbine,
I know I'm on the dying line.

Michael (age 13)

## The Kirn

Auld Tam McDougall was a weak and skinny plooman. He wore big tackity boots, lang an' baggy troosers and an auld, torn overcoat.

That nicht it wis the yearly Kirn an' Tam made up his mind tae gang. It was a braw Kirn, held by auld Jock Dow, fa' wis fair happy wi' the hairst bein' in. Lang afore mid-nicht, auld Tam wis awready drunk and wis tryin' tae dae the Hielin' Fling, but aye fa'in' doon on the flair. Doon allo the coos were wondrin' whit wis goin' on up there. Jock an' a freend gether'd puir Tam fae the flair an' threw him doon the stairs. Tam wisna' very pleased aboot this an' tried tae get back up, but he wis that drunk that he coodna' get back up, so he had tae gae hame.

But back inside the ither folk were havin' a rare auld time, wi' dancin' aboot on the flair. Some were throwin' sweeties at een anither. This lasted a' nicht. Man, whit a nicht it wis. We were fair sad when it had tae stop.

Tommy (age 11)

## The Declaration

T'was o'er six hunner years gone past
When Robert th' Bruce cam by,
Tae sign the scroll for Scotland's richt,
For the freedom o' Scotia for aye.

The Declaration was tae be signed
In the Abbey at Aberbrothock.
Mony great men were there tae see
Bernard de Linton hand roon' the scroll.

Now Scotland is free and worries are rare
A Scotsman is now a man
Because sae lang ago they focht,
Tae keep their Scottish land.

Valerie (age 12)

# Legends
# and Folklore

## LEGENDS

A legend is an old traditional tale, usually containing many strange
and fantastic characters and deeds.

## MONSTERS

### *The Wild Beast of Barriesdale*

In the parish of Knoydart there is a loch which because of its dark,
deep and gloomy waters is called Loch Hourn (Gaelic for Hell).
This loch was for long believed to be haunted by 'The Wild Beast of
Barriesdale'. It was said to have only three legs – two in front and
one behind. Nothing could divert it from its direct route. It jumped
over fences and even crofts; neither river nor loch could stop its
course.

In the year 1880, this monster was encountered by a crofter who
lived on the shores of the loch. He described it as a huge, three-
legged beast with gigantic wings, which he saw flying towards him
across the hills of Knoydart. Up to the time of his death, this man
used to tell how he was pursued by the creature as far as his cottage,
where he just succeeded in slamming the door in its face.

## *Peerifool*

There were once a king and queen in Rousay who had three daughters. The King died, and the queen was living in a small house with her daughters. They kept a cow and a kail-yard; they found their cabbage was all being taken away, and the eldest daughter said to the queen that she would take a blanket about her and would sit and watch what was going away with the kail. So when night came she went to watch.

In a short time a very big giant came into the yard; he began to cut the kail and throw it into a big cubby. So he cut till he had it well filled. The princess was always asking him why he was taking her mother's kail. He was saying to her, if she was not quiet he would take her too.

As soon as he had filled his cubby he took her by a leg and an arm and threw her on top of his cubby and away he went with her. When he got home he told her what work she had to do. She had to milk the cow and put her up to the hills called Bloodfield, and then she had to take wool, and wash and tease it and comb and card, and spin and make claith.

When the giant went out she milked the cow and put her to the hills. Then she put on a pot and made some porridge to herself. As she was supping it, a great many peerie yellow-headed folk came running, calling out to give them some. She said:

> Little for one, and less for two,
> And never a grain have I for you.

When she came to work the wool, none of that work could she do at all. The giant came home at night and found she had not done her work. He took her and began at her head, and peeled the skin off all the way down her back and over her feet. Then he threw her on the couples among the hens.

The same adventure befell the second girl and she found herself with her sister amongst the hens, unable to speak or come down.

The third night the youngest princess said she would take a blanket about her and go to watch what had gone away with her sisters. Ere long, in came the giant with the big cubby, and began to cut the kail. She was asking why he was taking her mother's kail. He was saying if she would not be quiet he would take her too.

He took her by a leg and an arm and threw her on top of his cubby, and carried her away.

Next morning he gave her some work as he had given her sisters. When he was gone she milked the cow and put her to the high hills. Then she put on the pot and made some porridge to herself. When the peerie yellow-headed folk came asking for some she told them to get something to sup with. Some got heather cows and some got broken dishes; some got one thing and some another and they all got some of her porridge. After they were all gone a peerie yellow-headed boy came in and asked her if she had any work to do; he could do any work with wool. She said she had plenty but would never be able to pay him for it. He said all he was asking was for her to tell him his name. She thought that would be easy to do, and gave him the wool.

When it was getting dark an old woman came in to ask her for lodging. The princess said she couldn't give her that, but asked her if she had any news. But the old woman had none, and went away to lie out.

There was a high knowe near the place and the old woman sat under it for shelter. She found it very warm. She climbed slowly up and when she came to the top she heard someone inside saying, "Tease, teasers, tease; card, carders, card; spin, spinners, spin, for Peerifool, Peerifool is my name."

There was a crack in the knowe and light coming out. She looked in and saw a great many peerie folk working, and a peerie yellow-headed boy running round and calling out what she had heard. The old woman thought she would get lodging if she went to give this news, so she came back and told the princess the whole of it.

The princess went on saying "Peerifool, peerifool" till the yellow-headed boy came with all the wool made into claith. He asked what his name was, and she guessed names, and he jumped about and said no. At last she said, "Peerifool is your name," and he threw down the wool and ran away, very angry.

As the giant was coming home he met a great many peerie yellow-headed folk, some with their eyes hanging out on their cheeks, and some with their tongues hanging on their breasts. He asked them what was the matter. They told him it was working so hard pulling wool so fine. He said he had a good wife at home, and if she was safe never would he allow her to do any work again.

When he came home she was safe, and had a great many webs lying all ready, and he was very kind to her.

Next day, when he was out she found her sisters, and took them down from the couples. She put the skin on their backs again, and she put her eldest sister in a cazy, and put all the fine things she could find with her, and put grass on top.

When the giant came home she asked him to take the cazy to her mother with some food for the cow. He was so pleased with her he would do anything for her, and took it away. Next day she did the same with her other sister. She told him she would have the last of the food she had to send to her mother for the cow ready next night, but she herself was going a bit from home, and would leave it for him. She got into the cazy with all the fine things she could find, and covered herself with grass. He took the cazy and carried it to the queen's house. She and her daughters had a big boiler of boiling water ready. They couped it about him when he was under the window, and that was the end of the giant.

(From *A Forgotten Heritage* by Hannah Aitken)

## Jock and his Bagpipes

There was a lad called Jock, and one day he said to his mother: "Mother, I'm going away to seek my fortune."

"Very well, my son," said she. "Take the sieve and the dish to the well. Fetch home some water, and I'll make you a bannock. If you fetch home a lot of water, you'll get a large bannock, but if you fetch home little water, you'll get a wee one."

So he took the sieve and the dish, and went to the well.

When he came to the well, he saw a wee bird sitting on the hillside, and when it saw Jock with the sieve and the dish, it said:

Stuff it with moss,
and clog it with clay,
And that will carry
The water away.

"Oh, you stupid creature!" said Jock. "Do you think I'm going to do as you bid me? Na, na!"

So the water ran out of the sieve, and he took home a little water in the dish. His mother baked a wee bannock to him, and he went away to seek his fortune.

After he had been on the road a short while, the wee bird came to him. "Give me a piece of your bannock," it said, "and I'll give you a feather out of my wing to make bagpipes for yourself."

"I'll not," said Jock. "It's all your fault I've such a wee bannock, and it's not enough for myself."

So the bird flew away. Jock went far, and far, and farther than I can say. When he came to the King's house, he went in and asked for work.

"What can you do?" said the Housekeepers.

"I can sweep a house, take out ashes, wash dishes and keep cows," said he.

"Can you keep hares?"

"I don't know," said he, "but I'll try."

They told him that if he kept hares, and brought them all home at night, he could wed the King's daughter. If he did not fetch them all home, he would be hanged.

So, in the morning, Jock set out with four and twenty hares and one cripple. He was very hungry, for he had only had a wee bannock, so he caught the crippled hare, killed it, roasted it and ate it. When the other hares saw this, they all ran away.

When he came home at night without any hares, the King was very angry, and ordered him to be hanged.

Now, his mother had another son, and he was also called Jock.

"Mother," said he, one day, "I'm going to seek my fortune."

"Very well, son," said she. "Take the sieve and the dish to the well, and fetch home some water. If you fetch home a lot of water, you shall have a large bannock. If you fetch home little water. You'll get a wee one."

So he took the sieve and the dish, and went to the well. And there he saw a wee bird sitting on the hillside. When it saw Jock with the sieve and the dish, it said:

> Stuff it with moss,
> And clog it with clay,
> And that will carry
> The water away.

"Ay, my bonny bird," said Jock, "I will."

So he stuffed the sieve with moss and clogged it with clay, and was able to fetch home a lot of water. His mother baked him a very large bannock, and away he went to seek his fortune.

After he was on the road a bit, the bird came to him.

"Give me a piece of your bannock," it said, "and I'll give you a feather out of my wing to make bagpipes for yourself."

"Ay, my bonny bird, I will," said he, "for it was you who helped me to get such a large bannock."

He gave the bird a piece of his bannock.

"Pull a feather out of my wing," said the bird, and make bagpipes for yourself."

"Na, na! I'll not pull a feather, for it'll hurt you."

"Just do as I bid," said the bird.

So Jock pulled a feather out of its wing, made the bagpipes and went along the road playing a merry tune.

He went far, and far, and farther than I can tell. When he came to the King's house, he went in and asked for work.

"What can you do?" said the Housekeepers.

"I can sweep a house, take out ashes, wash the dishes and keep cows," said he.

"Can you keep hares?"

"I don't know, but I'll try," said he.

63

They told him if he could keep hares, and fetch them all home at night, he would win the King's daughter, but if he did not fetch them all home, he would be hanged.

Next morning he set out with four and twenty and a crippled one. Jock played them such a bonny tune on his bagpipes that they all danced round him and never left his side.

That night he fetched them all home. The crippled one could not walk, so he took it up in his arms and carried it.

The King was very well pleased, and he gave him his daughter, and Jock was King when the old King died.

(From *The Well at the World's End* by Norah & William Montgomerie)

## The Laird of Co

One sunny morning the good Laird of Co was taking a stroll about his castle grounds; and there came to him a wee laddie, dangling a tin pannikin on his arm.

"If ye please, Laird of Co," says the wee laddie, "my mither lies sick in the bed, and if ye could spare her a drop of ale, I'm thinking 'twould do her good."

"Why of course she shall have some ale," said the Laird of Co. "Go to the kitchen, laddie, and ask the butler to fill your pannikin full with the best ale in my cellar. Say I sent you."

So off runs the wee laddie to the castle kitchen, finds the butler, and gives him the laird's message. The butler takes the laddie down to the wine cellar. Well, well, the best did the laird say? That would be in the barrel that was specially kept for the laird's own drinking.

"A pity," thought the butler, "to waste that on a poor woman who wouldn't know the best from the worst!" However, the master's orders must be obeyed, and after all, that little pannikin wouldn't hold more than a pint, if that.

So the butler took the pannikin from the wee laddie, held it under the tap of the barrel with one hand, and turned the tap with the other hand. Out came the ale in a golden stream, ripple, ripple,

ripple, ripple: and out it came, and out it came – but what was this? The barrel was swiftly emptying itself, but the little pannikin was not yet half full! Plague on it, this was sheer witchery; the laddie must be a bogle, and his mother no better! The butler didn't like it – no, he did not! "Here take your ale and be off with ye," says he to the wee laddie.

"But my pannikin is not full yet," says the wee laddie.

"It's full enough," says the butler. "It's emptied the cask!"

"The laird said I was to have my pannikin full," says the wee laddie.

"And how am I to fill it if it won't fill?" cries the butler. "It's witchery! Away with you and take your witchery some place else!"

"The laird said I was to have my pannikin full," said the wee laddie again.

"Be off, ere I give you a clout!" says the butler.

"The laird said I was to have my pannikin full," said the wee laddie.

No. He wouldn't budge. So the butler hurried off to tell the Laird of Co that he had a bogle in the cellar.

But the laird only laughed. "I did tell the laddie he should have his pannikin full," said he. "And have it full he shall, if it takes all the ale in my cellar. So go back and broach another cask."

The butlers teeth were chattering, and his hair was standing on end.

"I'm afeared the wee bogle bodes us no good," said he.

"Pooh!" said the Laird of Co. "Do as you're bid."

So the butler went down to the cellar again, and broached another cask. "Give us that damned pannikin of yours," says he to the wee laddie.

The laddie handed him the pannikin. What happened this time?

Scarcely had the butler held it under the tap of the newly broached barrel, when the pannikin was full to the brim. The laddie took the full pannikin and off with him: up out of the cellar, and through the castle grounds, skipping along past the Laird of Co, with a "Good day to ye!" and so out of sight behind a copse of elders. And though the good laird asked this one and the other one about the laddie and his mother, thinking they might be in need of help, not one of those he asked had ever heard tell of them, much less set eyes on them.

Well, the years passed; and there came a day when war broke out between the laird's country and a foreign country. The Laird of Co put on his armour, and crossed the sea to fight for his country, like the brave man he was. But though he fought valiantly, he was taken prisoner, and shut up in jail, and condemned to death.

So there he was, on the night before his execution, lying on the dank floor of his prison cell, and thinking of his home: of his castle and his pleasant grounds, and the rivers and lochs and mountains of his beloved country which he would never see again. And there came into his mind a memory of one sunny morning, of himself strolling on the green lawn in front of his castle, of the daisies winking in the sun and wind, and of a wee laddie stepping towards him over the daisied grass dangling a pannikin on his arm.

Such a clear picture the laird had of that wee laddie – he could almost see him now . . . almost see him? But he was seeing him!

The door of the prison cell had opened without a sound, and there was the wee laddie stepping noiselessly over the straw-littered floor with his finger to his lip.

And the wee laddie whispered:

> Laird o' Co,
> Rise and go!
> If ye'd be free,
> Follow me!

Like a man in a dream the Laird of Co got to his feet and followed the wee laddie out through the open door, down one long passage, and another long passage, through locked doors that opened at the wee laddie's touch, past prison guards who lay snoring at their posts, out into the prison yard, and through the great barred gates that swung open noiselessly to let them pass.

"Now, Laird o' Co," said the wee laddie, "get ye on my back."

"I get on your back, my little one?"

"Yes on my back."

"I am surely dreaming," said the Laird of Co, as he set his long legs across the wee laddie's back.

> For never waking one so tall
> Could ride upon a back so small!

But ride upon that back he did, and away went the wee laddie over the land, over the water, over the moors, over the mountains, and never stopped till he set the laird down in front of his own castle, on his own green lawn, where the daisies were winking in the sun and wind.

The wee laddie was laughing. He looked up at the Laird of Co, and said:

> Ae good turn deserves anither,
> I to ye, ye to my mither.

And with that he gave a hop and a skip, and vanished.

Nor did the Laird of Co ever see that wee laddie again.

(From *Scottish Folk Tales* by Ruth Manning-Sanders)

## My Own Self

"Percy Armstrong, get to your bed."

"No!"

"Percy Armstrong, do you hear what I say?"

"Aye. I hear."

"Well then, are you going to your bed?"

"No!"

'Percy Armstrong, if you don't go to your bed, the old fairy-wife will get you."

"Let her try!"

"Percy Armstrong, if you don't get to your bed, I will go to mine and leave you."

"Och – go then!"

So Percy Armstrong's mother went to bed, and left the little laddie Percy sitting on the kitchen floor in front of the fire.

When he hadn't been sitting there very long when he heard a huffle-wuffle in the chimney, and down on to the hearth jumped a teeny-tiny fairy girl, no bigger than a doll, with silvery hair, and grass-green eyes, and cheeks the colour of a linnet's breast.

"Oh!" said Percy. And, "Oh" says he again. "And what might they be calling you?"

"Just my own self," said the teeny-tiny fairy girl, in a sweet little chirruping teeny-tiny voice. "And what will they be calling you?"

"Just my own self, too," says Percy.

And they began to play together.

The teeny-tiny fairy girl knew some fine games. She took up the ashes from the hearth in her teeny-tiny hands, and made those ashes

68

into teeny-tiny animals and birds that ran about, and flew, and talked and sang. She made teeny-tiny trees, and teeny-tiny houses, and teeny-tiny people, not an inch high, who looked out of the doors of their houses, and walked here and there, and chatted one to the other in oh such teeny-tiny voices! Percy laughed and clapped his hands; he couldn't have enough of such games.

And just think – if he had gone to bed, as his mother had bidden him, he would have missed all this!

Well now, by and by the fire burned low, and the light from it was getting dim. Percy couldn't see so well what the teeny-tiny fairy girl was doing. So he took up a stick and stirred the coals; and there – if a hot cinder didn't go and fall on to the teeny-tiny girl's teeny-tiny foot!

Oh, oh, oh – what a screech she gave! It was like all the winds in the world whistling through a teeny-tiny keyhole.

That screech gave Percy a fright! He had just taken a leap to hide himself under the table, when a huge great voice sounded in the chimney:

"What's to do there? Who is it screeching?"

"Just my own self," blubbered the teeny-tiny girl. "My . . . my f-foot's burned sore, with a h-hot c-cinder!"

"And who did that?" Roared the huge great voice, very angry, in the chimney.

"Just my own self, too," whimpered the fairy girl.

"Then if you did it your own self," shouted the voice in the chimney, "what's the use of making such a fash about it?"

And Percy, peeping from under the table, saw a great hand, on the end of a long skinny arm, poking out from down the chimney. Percy could still hear the squealing. Quicker than quick he ran to his bed, and dived down under the blankets.

Next night, when his mother told him it was time for bed, Percy was willing enough to go. For who knows what might have happened when she of the great hand and arm got to know the truth of the matter?

(From *Scottish Folk-Tales* by Ruth Manning-Sanders)

# WITCHES

## *Stein Veg of Tarbet*

Stein Veg lived in a lonely cottage on the shores of the Moray Firth.

She was an old 'wise-woman', said to have power over winds and waves. One day some fishermen, who were storm-stayed nearby, decided to test her magic powers and see if she could sell them a favourable wind.

One of the men, therefore, visited the old, bent woman in her cottage.

The smoke from her peat-fire half-blinded him as she threw handfuls of dried seaweed on to the fire and muttered strange words to herself. When the fisherman asked her to sell him a fair wind she asked him to bring her the water-stoup from his boat.

On his return, the fisherman found in the cottage all the things associated with witches: a black cat, a raven on the rafters overhead, bones and a bundle of weeds. The fire had been piled high with dry turf, and ghostly shadows flickered on the walls and floor.

Stein Veg took the water-stoup from the fisherman and told him to wait outside.

Strange lights and shadows could be seen through the window before Stein Veg came out again and gave the fisherman back the stoup with a wisp of straw in its neck. "You can sail at dawn," she told him, "but take care you do not remove the wisp of straw until you are safely home."

Next morning the wind had dropped; only a gentle breeze blew from the north-west. The boat set sail. One of the crew wondered what the old woman had put in the water-stoup, but the fisherman who had been to Stein Veg's cottage urged his friends to wait till they were safely back in Cromarty Bay before satisfying their curiosity. The rest of the crew laughed at him and one man pulled the wisp of straw out of the neck of the stoup. There was only water inside. Furious, the man threw the straw into the sea, saying that Stein Veg had deceived them.

At once the sky darkened, the wind suddenly swung round and huge waves broke over the decks as the little boat plunged and tossed in the rough sea. The wild storm lasted for twenty-four hours and was the fiercest in that part of Scotland that anyone could remember. The boat was driven on to the rocks and all the crew were lost, except for one man – the fisherman who bought the fair wind.

## Tam O'Shanter

In olden times, people were much more superstitious than they are today. Things which they did not understand often frightened them and disasters such as the failure of crops, outbreaks of fire, people falling and injuring themselves, were often blamed on 'witches'.

Witches and spirits appear not only in the legends of Scotland, but also in many of the songs and poems of old. Perhaps the most famous poem dealing with supernatural events, is 'Tam O' Shanter' by Robert Burns.

Tam O' Shanter on his way home from a drunken party sees lights blazing over the old deserted kirkyard of Alloway. He creeps up to investigate, and sees a horrifying sight:

> Warlock an' witches in a dance;
> Nae cotillion brent new frae France,
> But hornpipes, jigs, strathspeys, an' reels,
> Put life an' mettle in their heels:
> At winnock-bunker in the east,
> There sat Auld Nick, in shape o' beast;
> A towzie tyke, black grim, an' large,
> To gie them music was his charge;
> He screwed the pipes and gart them skirl,
> Till roof and rafters a' did dirl.
> Coffins stood round, like open presses,
> That shaw'd the dead in their last dresses;
> And (by some dev'lish cantraip sleight)
> Each in its cauld hand held a light:

71

By which heroic Tam was able
To note upon the haly table,
A murderer's banes in gibbet airns;
Twa span-lang, wee, unchristen'd bairns;
A thief, new cutted frae a rape –
Wi' his last gasp his gab did gape;
Five tomahawks, wi' bluid red-rusted;
Five scimitars wi' murder crusted;
A garter, which a babe had strangled;
A knife a father's throat had mangled,
Whom his ain son o' life bereft,
The grey hairs yet stack to the heft;
Wi' mair o' horrible an' awfu',
Which ev'n to name would be unlawfu'.

Tam watches as the witches reel and dance to the bagpipe music played by the devil. Most of the witches are old and ugly, but one is young and pretty and, forgetful of danger, Tam calls out to her.

*Tam o' Shanter* by Walter Geikie

In a flash all is dark and the witches and spirits pour out of the old kirkyard to chase Tam, who quickly clambers on to his horse Meg.

Tam rides out at the utmost speed for he knows that if he can reach the middle of the brig over the stream he will be safe – for spirits cannot cross running water. Tam and Meg reach the brig and are nearly over when the young witch catches Meg's tail, which comes off, leaving the horse with only a stump.


## BANSHEES

## *The Three Banshees*

There once lived in western Skye, a shepherd by name of Norman Macsweyn. One day, when he was out on the great stretches of moorland tending his sheep, a kindly neighbour called to see his wife.

"Why, Mistress Macsweyn," she said, when the door was opened to her, "upon my word, you do look tired."

"I have done a hard day's work, neighbour," replied the shepherd's wife, "cleaning, washing, baking bread. And the baby is ailing, she has cried all day." She wiped a weary hand across her brow.

"Well get you to yon bed and rest awhile," said her friend. "I'll stay and look after the bairn."

The shepherd's wife gladly accepted the kind offer, went to her bed, lay down on it and closed her eyes. The neighbour took up the whimpering babe from its cot, sat down by the fire and began crooning softly to the child. Soon the baby ceased crying, and the warmth from the fire and the quiet in the room sent the good neighbour to sleep.

But the mother, although dozing happily, was not asleep, and, on opening her eyes for a second, she was surprised to see three funny little women grouped around her sleeping friend and the baby.

73

They were shadowy, grey, ugly little women and, although they were standing in front of the fire, she was able to see the flames through them.

They made no noise when they entered the house, and were making none now. Mistress Macsweyn was frightened. Could these be banshees?

She had often heard of them, but never seen any before. She stayed motionless on the bed. The little women were whispering. She strained to hear what they were saying.

"Take up the babe, and we'll away with it," said the eldest of the little women, who was standing nearest the bed.

The second banshee spoke, and her voice was like a thin, high note played on an old fiddle. "Is it not a shame, sister, to rob the poor woman Macsweyn of this one babe when you already have had so many of her children?"

The shepherd and his wife had lost many babies through sickness.

"Yes, indeed," agreed the third banshee. "Have pity on the wretched woman."

"When have we ever had pity on anyone?" cried out the senior banshee. "Pity is a word we do not know."

Still her sisters pleaded with her to spare the child, until at last she agreed.

"Well, we'll not take the child away," she said, "but this I declare: when that little piece of peat that is burning in the hearth shall be burned out, the child will surely die."

The banshees crept out of the house, moving like a cloud of mist away across the moors to no-one knows where.

The neighbour was still asleep, but as soon as the banshees had gone, the mother leapt up from her bed, seized a large jug of water that was standing on a table nearby, and poured it over the fire. There was a spluttering and a hissing as the fire went out. She snatched from the hearth the sodden piece of peat to which the banshees referred, and, wrapping it carefully in a cloth, she hid it in a small wooden chest she kept under the bed, happy in the thought that she had saved the life of her little daughter, who was already beginning to stir on the neighbour's lap.

The years passed as swiftly as the flight of a bird. The little girl – whose name was Oighrig – grew into a lovely young woman. And, as was to be expected, she met a young man with whom she fell in love, and they became engaged to be married. In those days, in the Isles, the bride-to-be did not attend church from the day she was betrothed until the day she was married. So it happened that one Sunday morning, Norman Macsweyn and his wife set out early on the twelve-mile walk to church, leaving Oighrig behind in the house. She busied herself, preparing the dinner for her parents when they should return. The meat was in the oven and the vegetables simmering in the cooking pots, so she looked around for something else to occupy her time. But her mother had left the house clean and tidy, and there was nothing else to do. She sat down by the fire, awaiting her parent's return. She was restless and bored. It was a dismal day. The wind blowing and the rain heavy.

If there was nothing to do in the house, it was impossible to do anything outside. Oighrig sighed.

"Oh dear, I wish I had something to do," she murmured. "It will be hours before Mother and Father get back, and everyone's in church except me, so there aren't likely to be any callers."

At that moment, her eyes rested on the little wooden chest that her mother always kept under her bed. It was a strange thing about that chest; she had never been allowed to touch it, let alone play with it or look inside it. The only time – many years ago – that she had dared to put her hand on the lid, her mother had smacked and scolded her. The memory was still very clear. What was so precious about the box, she wondered? What did it contain that her mother should guard it so carefully? Oihgrig suspected that even her father did not know the answer. She was tempted. She glanced out of the window, but there was no sign of her parents. Now was her chance to find out the secret of the chest which had puzzled her off and on all her life.

She knew she was doing wrong and that her mother would be angry if she found out. Nevertheless, she stealthily pulled out the chest and lifted the lid. As far as she could judge, the chest was full of odds and ends, none of them very valuable. Oighrig sat cross-legged

75

on the floor and took out the things, one by one. There were a few pieces of cheap jewellery, of a kind her mother might have won at a fair some time; and there were one or two fine lawn handkerchiefs, edged with lace, and a white slipper (that her mother had worn at her wedding perhaps); there was a jar of ointment, a broken hammer, some reels of coloured thread, some odd scraps of material. The chest contained nothing of value, nor did it seem to contain, as far as Oighrig could see, anything that could possibly harm her. It did, however, contain one rather surprising item. At the bottom, she found a piece of cloth wrapped round, of all things, a bit of peat. Her mother must be mad to keep such a silly thing. She supposed it had got there by mistake. She put back the other articles tidily but the peat she threw carelessly on the fire, knowing no other good use to which it might be put.

The peat smouldered; poor Oighrig began to feel ill. By the time her parents had returned from church, she was too weak to get up and greet them.

"Why, Oighrig, my daughter," cried her father, "what ails you?"

The mother saw the chest, pulled out from under the bed; Oighrig had not had the strength to replace it.

"Oighrig!" cried out the wretched woman, "have you touched anything in this chest? Anything at all?"

"I looked at the contents; I'm sorry, Mother," replied the girl.

"Did you put back everything?" asked Mistress Macsweyn rummaging wildly through the chest. "All but the piece of peat, which I put on the fire; everything mother dear, but the peat. I did not think you would want the peat." The mother let out a cry of despair and, as the peat the banshee had cursed gave a last little flicker, so life left the body of Oighrig Macsweyn.

(From *Scottish Legendary Tales* by Elizabeth Sheppard-Jones)

## *The Pretty Spotted Pig*

Long ago and ever before there were roads, trains or planes, Perthshire was a forest and wild beasts roamed the countryside, such as it was. People spoke of strange animals that took children screaming from their beds and ate sheep whole and alive. They sang of the brave knights who killed beasts and wore their heads as a crest.

Not all the beasts were killed or banished. Those left were more than tame emblems of strength, and knights had plenty to worry them. Sir Lionel was a knight at court. He and the other knights lived well enough, eating from a long oak table with gold candlesticks and sleeping in beds adorned with gold and covered in feather down. Their ladies were the fairest of women, with a pale and brooding beauty. The knights delighted in hunting and, with their hawks and hounds, roamed the great forests.

One day Sir Lionel rode across many moors and mosses to the edge of the forest, where he met a lady. She was sitting beneath a tree, her eyes wet with many sore tears. Though he was a brave knight, Sir Lionel was disturbed by the weeping woman and did not know how to comfort her. In time, when the lady had ceased weeping, she told him her trouble. There was a great boar inside the forest and her lord and some of his knights had come across the beast while it was sleeping. In a fury the wild boar had killed her lord and his knights, despite their skill at arms. Since that time she had been alone on the edge of the forest.

Being a fearless knight, Sir Lionel set out to kill the boar.

He searched for two days before he came across its tracks; he followed them, and arrived in a clearing. Snores filled the glade. There was neither beast nor bird in sight; a few flies buzzed and circled round the boar's great snout.

Sir Lionel hurled his lance at the boar's heaving heart; his aim was poor and only the shaft stunned the beast. He drew his sword and prepared to meet the onrush. The boar was not dazed for long.

It stamped the ground, lowered its head and charged the knight. They fought a long and bitter struggle before Sir Lionel plunged the boar's heart. But he was sorely wounded by the time the fight was through.

Unknown to Sir Lionel, the boar belonged to a giant who was very fond of his pet, and was, naturally, upset when he heard of its death.

The giant came to Sir Lionel in a rage, and told him he must forfeit his hawk, hounds, the little finger of his right hand, and finally his lady, to atone for the death of the pet boar. Sir Lionel was in no condition to consider such a demand, so he refused it.

He was allowed thirty days to heal his wounds and repair his body. Then the giant demanded that Sir Lionel return to the forest prepared to meet his demands or fight until death. He took Sir Lionel's lady as security for the knight's return. When the lady arrived, Sir Lionel was not at all pleased to see her go with the giant, but she was sure her knight would rescue her and went without tears.

At the end of the month the salves, soups, herbs and ointments which Sir Lionel had been given healed his wounds and strengthened him. He returned to the forest and called the giant from his cave. The two fought long and hard until Sir Lionel eventually overcame the huge man and killed him, just as he had killed the boar.

Exhausted and bloody, he returned to the cave to collect his lady. But there Sir Lionel got another fright. The giant had a wife, who was a wild woman. She brooded long and often and filled the giant's cave with words. When she saw it was the knight who returned, and not her husband, she flew at Sir Lionel in a wild, wild rage. "You've slain my pretty spotted pig and now my darling giant," she cried, screaming like a gull, she swung at Sir Lionel with a wood chopper. The knight side-stepped her axe and cleaved the woman with his sword.

So Sir Lionel and his lady returned to the castle. They sat at the long oak table and told of their adventure. No one had told what happened to the lady whose tears started it all. Life was no worse for her. In time we accept misfortune and look for better luck to follow.

Especially when there are no boars, giants or wild women to worry about.

(From *A Cuckoo's Nest* by Carl Macdougall)

FOLKLORE

## The Clever Apprentice

A shoemaker once employed an apprentice.

"What would you call me when you speak to me?" he asked.

"I would call you master," said the boy.

"No," said the shoemaker, "you must call me Master of all Masters. What would you call my trousers?"

"Oh I would just call them trousers."

"No, you must call them strontifiers. What would you call my wife?"

"I would call her Mistress."

"No, you must call her the fair Lady Permoumadam. And what would you call my son?"

"I would call him Johnny."

"No, you must call him John the Great. What would you call the cat?"

"I would just call him Pussy."

"No, you must call him Great Carle Gropius, what would you call the fire?"

"Oh I would call it the fire."

"No, you must call it Fire Evangelist. And the peatstack?"

"I would call that the peatstack."

"No, you must call it Mount Potago. What would you call the well?"

"I would just call it the well."

"No, you must call it the Fair Fountain. Last of all, what would you call the house?"

"I would call it the house."

"No, you must call it the Castle of Mungo."

Then the shoemaker told the lad that the first time he had occasion to use all these words at once his apprenticeship would be at an end.

The apprentice was not long in making an occasion. One morning, after he had lit the fire, he lit a few papers. He put them on to the peatstack and set it on fire.

80

"Master of all Masters," shouted the apprentice, "start up and jump into your strontifers, and call upon John the Great and the fair Lady Permoumadam, for the Great Carle Gropius has got hold of Fire Evangelist and he's out to Mount Potago, and if you don't get help from the Fair Fountain the whole Castle of Mungo will burn to the ground."

And that was the end of the apprenticeship.

(From *A Forgotten Heritage* by Hannah Aitken)

## *The Left-Handed Screw-Driver*

My first day at work was a long one. I dashed round the office, flushed with a new freedom and alive with an excitement of discovery that soon wore off.

Halfway through the afternoon, my boss said: "Do you know where the stores are? Right then; off you go and ask for a long stand."

The storeman's face was split by a cigarette which dangled unsucked from a corner of his mouth. The ash drooped like a willow branch and the front of his brown overall was covered with grey powder. His eye was half-closed, permanently suspicious.

"You new here?" he said. "Aye, that's right, you will be. Just wait here." Off he went, shuffling round the stores, checking his shelves and ticking their contents on a clip-board crowded with paper. His pencil was blunt and he occasionally licked it with his tongue as if to sharpen the lead. Magically, his cigarette was never disturbed.

Impatient and restless, I caught his open eye. "How about that long stand I asked for?"

"Well – you've been standing here for half an hour. Isn't that long enough?" I was lucky. Some have been sent for tartan paint, a bucket of steam, a soft-headed hammer. The bubble for a spirit level or a host of other plausible impossibilities. Someone I know was asked to fetch a left-handed screw-driver and returned with – just a screw-driver. "If you try it with your left hand, it works," he told the boss, proudly.                    (From *A Cuckoo's Nest* by Carl Macdougall)

# Ballads and Folk Songs

## BALLADS

The first ballads were like stories. They were told by merchants and travellers who moved all over the countryside on their travels.

Long ago people did not often move far from their villages and it was an exciting event when a merchant or traveller passed through a village or called on a lonely farm. In those days, before newspapers, radio or television had been heard of, news of events, stories and songs were all passed by word of mouth.

Story ballads would sometimes tell of famous battles, love stories or tragedies, while others would deal with fairies, witches and supernatural events.

In the nineteenth century the famous Scottish writer, Sir Walter Scott, collected a large number of such stories and had them printed for the first time. If this had not been done perhaps many might have been lost for ever.

These ballads have been popular, first with listeners, then with readers – for hundreds of years.

Ballads are still being written whenever there is a story or event that catches the imagination of writers, singers and ordinary folk. (See page 85.)

# Twa Corbies

As I was walking all alane,
I heard twa corbies making a mane;
The tane unto the t'other say,
'Where sall we gang and dine to-day?'

'In behint yon auld fail dyke,
I wot there lies a new-slain knight;
And naebody kens that he lies there,
But his hawk, his hound, and lady fair.

'His hound is to the hunting gane,
His hawk to fetch the wild-fowl hame,
His lady's ta'en another mate,
So we may make our dinner sweet.

'Ye'll sit on his white hause-bane,
And I'll pike out his bonny blue een;
Wi' ae lock o' his gowden hair
We'll theek our nest when it grows bare.

'Mony a one for him makes mane,
But nane sall ken where he is gane;
O'er white banes, when they are bare,
The wind sall blaw for evermair.'


# The Wife of Usher's Well

There lived a wife at Usher's Well,
  And a wealthy wife was she!
She had three stout and stalwart sons,
  And sent them o'er the sea

They hadna been a week from her,
  A week but barely ane,
Whan word came to the carlin wife
  That her three sons were gane.

They hadna been a week from her,
　　A week but barely three,
Whan word came to the carlin wife
　　That her sons she'd never see.

'I wish the wind may never cease,
　　Nor fashes in the flood,
Till my three sons come hame to me,
　　In earthly flesh and blood.'

It fell about the Martinmas,
　　When nights are lang and mirk,
The carlin wife's three sons came hame,
　　And their hats were o' the birk.

It neither grew in syke nor ditch,
　　Nor yet in ony sheugh;
But at the gates o' Paradise,
　　That birk grew fair eneugh.

'Blow up the fire, my maidens,
　　Bring water from the well;
For a' my house shall feast this night,
　　Since my three sons are well.'

And she has made to them a bed,
　　She's made it large and wide,
And she's taen her mantle her about,
　　Sat down at the bedside.

Up then crew the red, red cock,
　　And up and crew the gray;
The eldest to the youngest said,
　　''Tis time we were away.'

The cock he hadna crawd but once,
　　And clapp'd his wings at a',
When the youngest to the eldest said,
　　'Brother we must awa,

'The cock doth craw, the day doth daw,
  The channerin worm doth chide;
Gin we be mist out o' our place,
  A sair pain we maun bide.

'Fare ye weel, my mother dear!
  Fareweel to barn and byre!
And fare ye weel, the bonny lass,
  That kindles my mother's fire!'

The controversy over the disappearance of the Stone of Destiny
in the 1950s inevitably resulted in the birth of a ballad – a very
humorous account of the problems encountered in acquiring,
maintaining and preserving stones of destiny.

## The Wee Magic Stane

O the Dean o' Westminster was a powerful man
He held a' the strings o' the state in his han'.
But wi' all this great business, it lost him his name,
Some rogues ran awa' wi' his wee magic stane.

*Chorus*  Sing Toorala oorala toorala lay.

Noo the stane had great poo'ers that c'd dae such a thing
For wi'oot it it seemed we'd be wantin' a king.
So he called in the polis and he gave this decree
Go and hunt oot the stane and return it tae me.

     Sing Toorala ...

Sae the polis went beetlin' way up tae the north
They hunted the Clyde and they hunted the Forth,
But the wild folk up yonder just kidded them a'
That they didnae believe it wis magic at a'.

     Sing Toorala ...

Noo the Provost o' Glesga, Sir Victor by name,
He wis verra pit oot when he heard o' the stane
So he ordered the statues that stand in George Square
That the High Church's masons might carve up yun there.

    Sing Toorala . . .

When the Dean o' Westminster wi' this was acquent
He sent for Sir Victor and made him this tent.
'Now it's no good you sending your statues down here'
Said the Dean, 'But you have given me a jolly good idea'.

    Sing Toorala . . .

So he quarried a stane of the very same stuff
And he dressed it all up till it looked like enough,
Then he sent for the press and announced that the stane
Had been found and returned to Westminster again.

    Sing Toorala . . .

When the reivers found oot what Westminster had done
They went aboot digging up stanes by the ton
And for each one they finished they entered the claim
That this wis the true and original stane.

    Sing Toorala . . .

But the cream o' the joke still remains to be telt,
For the bloke that was turning them aff on the belt
At the peak of production was so sorely pressed
That the real yin got bunged in alang wi' the rest.

    Sing Toorala . . .

So, if ever you come on a stane wi' a ring
Just sit yersel' doon and appoint yersel' king,
For theres nane would be able to challenge your claim
That you crowned yersel' king on the destiny stane.

    Sing Toorala . . .

# The Barring of the Door

There once lived an old man with his wife in a little cottage high up in the windy hills. Now one year, round about the merry season of Martinmas in November, the old woman set about making puddings. While she was busy boiling the puddings, both black and white, in a pan over the fire, the cold wind got up and seemed to blow from all directions at once round the cottage, and in through every crack and into every cranny. The old man, who was sitting in his chair, shivered in the draught, and thinking the outside door of the cottage porch must have blown open he said to his wife, 'Go out and bar the door'.

The old woman did not look up from her puddings, but said, 'My hands are busy at my work, husband, as you can see; and even if that door stays open for a hundred years, it won't be barred by me.'

Now the husband did not like this wilfulness in his wife, and he determined to be just as stubborn as she was, so he just sat in his chair and let the wind whistle round his feet. The old woman went on stirring her puddings, saying not a word, and when she had done she came and sat down opposite her husband. The old couple sat there looking at one another, growing colder and colder, while the wind howled through the house, but neither of them budged.

At last, the old man said to his wife, "I'll tell you what, wife. 'Let's make a pact – whichever one of us speaks first will get up and bar the door.' The wife agreed, and they sat there in the cold, glaring at one another, with their lips tight shut.

The evening drew on until midnight, and still they sat, neither of them saying a word. Now it happened that two travellers came riding over the hills.

When they saw the cottage, they thought they might seek shelter overnight. There were no lights in the cottage, but as the door was open, they went inside, and found the old couple sitting glumly by the dying fire. The travellers greeted the man and his wife politely, but the old pair made no reply.

'Is this a well-off house, or a poor one?' asked one of the gentlemen. And still neither husband nor wife answered.

The two gentlemen looked at each other, and then they looked round the room, and soon spotted the puddings simmering in the pan by the fire. They helped themselves, and one ate the black pudding and the other ate the white. The old woman nearly burst with fury, but still she kept her lips tight shut, because of her pact with her husband.

One of the gentlemen winked at the other, and said, 'Here friend, take my knife and shave off the old man's beard with it, and meantime I'll kiss his wife here, sour-faced though she is.'

'But what can I use for shaving water,' said the other, taking the knife, 'there's none in the house.'

'Just use the hot water the puddings were boiled in,' said the first gentleman, lifting the pan from the fire.

At this the old man could stand no more. He leapt to his feet in rage. 'What you rogues.' cried he, 'would you kiss my wife before my very eyes, and scald me with pudding-water!'

But before he could say any more, his wife jumped from the chair and laughed triumphantly. She danced a jig on the floor, crying, 'Husband, you were the first to speak – get up and bar the door!'

(From *True Thomas the Rhymer and other tales of the Lowland Scots* by Heather and Tom Scott)

## The Men o' the North

As I cam in by Peterheid
I saw it changin' sairly O,
For the tankers grey stand in the bay
And the oil is flowing rarely O.


*Chorus*
The men o' the north are a' gane gyte,
A gane gyte togither, O.
The derricks rise tae the northern skies,
And the past is gane for ever, O.

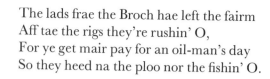

The lads frae the Broch hae left the fairm
Aff tae the rigs they're rushin' O,
For ye get mair pay for an oil-man's day
So they heed na the ploo nor the fishin' O.

I met wi a man frae Aiberdeen
That city aye sae bonnie O,
He said, "There's a spree by the dark North Sea,
And an affa smell o' money O.

What wad ye gie for the gowden sand
The whaup's cry in the morning O,
The rowan fair and the caller air
And the tide as it's gently turnin' O.

Sheila Douglas

# FOLK SONGS

Folk songs are like the ballads in that often they were not composed by one person, but produced by groups of people, perhaps working together. A large number of the folk songs of Scotland developed in the farm kitchens, fishing boats and factories in the cities; wherever people met and worked together. These songs are often about aspects of their everyday lives and occupations. Singing a folk song can be like singing a part of history. There are songs of love and marriage, songs of death and sorrow, songs of work and play of the common folk, songs about kings and queens, songs for children to sing, indeed songs about almost anything which the 'folk' or ordinary people come into contact with. One very interesting thing about folk songs is that each generation produces its own.

## STREET SONGS

The first folk songs here are children' street songs – to be sung out of pure enjoyment.

## *The Jeely Piece Song*

I'm a skyscraper wean, I live on the nineteenth flair,
But I'm no gaun oot tae play ony mair
Cos since we moved to Castlemilk, I'm wastin' away
Cos I'm gettin' one less meal every day.
Oh ye canny fling pieces oot a twenty storey flat
Seven hundred hungry weans'll testify to that,
If it's butter, cheese or jeely, if their breid is plain or pan,
The odds against it reachin' earth are ninety-nine tae wan.

Adam McNaughtan

Glasgow has a tradition of its own, familiar to, and half forgotten by, most of its inhabitants – the tradition of the street song. Nowhere else in Scotland has this form of real live 'folk' culture developed as it has in Glasgow.

These songs, which are mainly concerned with the effect of the words rather than the music, cover a narrow range of subjects, but reflect the considerable agility with words or 'patter' for which Glasgow is famed. These songs are sung by and are the progeny of the youngsters of Glasgow, and it is interesting to note how new verses are often invented for established songs.

> There is a happy land
> Down in Duke Street jail
> Where all the prisoners stand
> Tied tae a nail.
> Ham and eggs you ne'er shall see
> Dirty watter for yer tea
> There you live in misery
> God Save the Queen.

O ye canna shove yer granny aff a bus
O ye canna shove yer granny aff a bus
O ye canna shove yer granny, fer she's yer mammy's mammy
Ye canna shove yer granny aff a bus.

Ye can shove yer other granny aff a bus
Ye can shove yer other granny aff a bus
O ye can shove yer other granny, fer she's yer faither's mammy
Ye can shove yer other granny aff a bus.

# The Wark o' the Weavers

The Wark o' the Weavers is a song about the once flourishing trade
of handloom weaving. All over Scotland weaving was carried on,
very often in people's homes. In the song are mentioned a great
many other occupations, some of them, like the weavers, have
disappeared as a result of modern machinery.

We're a' met thegither here tae sit an' tae crack,
Wi oor glesses in oor hands an' oor wark upon oor back;
For there's nae a trade amang them a' can either mend or mak',
Gin it wasna for the wark o' the weavers.

*Chorus*

> If it wasna for the weavers what wad they do?
> They wadna hae claith made oot o' oor woo';
> They wadna hae a coat, neither black nor blue,
> Gin it wasna for the wark o' the weavers.

There's some folk independent o' ither tradesmen's wark
For women need nae barber an' dykers need nae clerk;
But there's no ane o' them but needs a coat an' a sark,
Na, they canna want the wark o' the weavers.

There's smiths an' there's wrights and there's mason chiels an' a',
There's doctors an' there's meenisters an' them that live by law,
An' oor freens that bide oot ower the sea in Sooth America,
An' they a' need the wark o' the weavers.

Oor sodgers an' oor sailors, od, we mak' them a' bauld
For gin they hadna claes, faith, they couldna fecht for cauld;
The high an' low, the rich an' puir – a'body young an' auld,
They a' need the wark o' the weavers.

So the weavin' is a trade that never can fail
Sae lang's we need ae cloot tae haud anither hale,
Sae let us a' be merry ower a bicker o' guid ale,
An' drink tae the health o' the weavers.

93

## The Apprentice Song

This Folk Song is all about the things an apprentice has to pay attention to. When a boy leaves school and takes up a trade he will come into contact with a whole new world. Sometimes when apprentices start work the older men will play tricks on them, like asking them to fetch a 'glass hammer' or to go for a 'long stand', but this is just harmless fun. In the serious job of learning, the experienced men show the apprentices the skills of their trade.

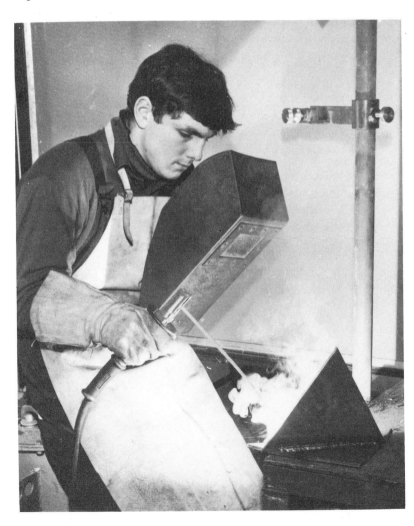

This song is about apprentice fitters who will work in the gasworks, helping millions of households to keep warm, and producing gas for the cookers to cook all the dinners waiting to be cooked.

Come on, lad, and bring your toolbag,
Keep your eyes peeled, use your head,
Fetch your footprints, spanners, chisels,
From now on you'll earn your bread.
Keep your eye on the older fitters,
They're the boys who know their stuff,
One day you will do their job.
If you're smart and keen enough.

Come on, boy, and take your place,
Among the men who serve the trade.
Scalers, cokers, valvesmen, stokers,
This is where the gas is made.
Keep your eye on old Fairweather,
Mind your gauge, you're on the town.
Turn her out bang-on four fifty.
Or you'll let the housewife down.

Wake up son, and mind your setting,
B range is the one to watch.
Number three is due for scaling,
See she don't get too much ash.
Mind your eye with that red hot poker,
Read your heat and see she's right,
Leave your range in decent order,
For the lads on shift tonight.

                              Ian Campbell

Making us laugh at ourselves and the way we live has for long been a popular topic among folk singers and writers.

 This song, which pokes fun at the double yellow lines for no parking, is based on the personal experience of the song writer's husband. The line mentioning the Bailie refers to the ironic fact that the first name on the first list of offenders against this new law in the city of Perth, was a local Bailie – and he was instrumental in introducing the double yellow lines system!

## *The Parking Song*

Now you've all heard about the train robbers
Who stole many thousands of pounds,
And the men who made off with the bullion
By daylight in old London town.

Well, I've got them all beaten hollow,
I've committed the worst crime on earth,
I'm the fellow who parked his old Hillman
On the wrong side of Scott Street in Perth.

I left it for full fifteen minutes
Just as brazen and bold as you like,
When I came back a bold traffic warden
Was standing there, ready to strike.

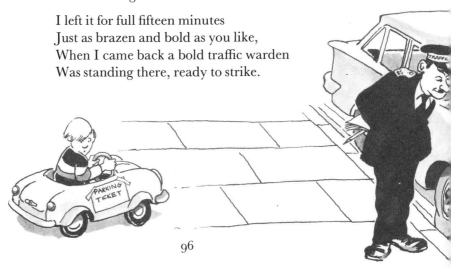

There's a wee notice up on the lamp post
Which, sat at the wheel, you can't spy
It's a terrible life for the motorist
So don't stop here, drive on right by.

When the police heard of my misdemeanour
They acted with great diligence,
Two uniformed men in a car came,
To charge me with this black offence.

The neighbours looked oot o' their windows
They thocht that I'd murdered my wife,
O little they knew, it was much worse,
I'd be lucky to get off with my life.

In due course I got a wee summons,
To appear on the fourth of September,
But when I got there, oh! what a surprise,
A Bailie was the first offender.

So if you come to the Fair City,
In Volkswagen or Chevrolet
Be careful when you see those yellow lines
And read what the notices say.

They don't mind if you've shot your grandmother
Or embezzled a million or two,
But if you're caught wrongfully parking
You've sure got it coming to you!

Sheila Douglas

Supplying barrels to the fish trade was but one of many outlets for the trade of the 'cooper' or barrel maker. Before the age of plastics, barrels were in demand for a wide range of products and the trade of 'coopering' a flourishing one. The Wee Cooper o' Fife does not deal with the work aspect of the cooper's trade, but is rather an amusing picture of a domestic problem.

## The Wee Cooper o' Fife

There was a wee cooper wha lived in Fife,
*Nickety nackety noo noo noo.*
And he hae gotten a gentle wife,
*Hey willie wallacky hoo John Dougal alane*
*quo rushety roo roo roo.*

She wadna bake nor she wadna brew
*Nickety nackety*, etc.
For the spoilin' o' her comely hue.
*Hey Willie Wallacky*, etc.

She wadna card nor she wadna spin
For the shamin' o' her gentle kin.

She wadna wash nor she wadna wring
For the spoilin' o' her gowden ring.

The cooper has gane to his woo' pack
He laid a sheep's-skin across his wife's back

I wadna thrash ye for your gentle kin
But I wad thrash my ain sheep's-skin.

A' ye wha hae gotten a gentle wife
Send ye for the wee cooper o' Fife.

# Proverbs
# and Sayings

The sayings on the map overleaf refer to something about the local areas from which they come. This is what they mean.

1. A piece of advice to those people living on the Moray Coast or Laigh: neither provoke hostility nor look for hospitality from neighbours in the Highlands.
2. Take away Aberdeen and its surroundings and there would be little of worth left, according to Aberdonians.
3. This saying refers to the fertile nature of Donside and the rugged and forested banks of the Dee.
4. Pig headed people should be left to their own devices.
5. The lands surrounding the crooked path of the River Forth are very fertile in contrast with the rocky nature of the Highlands.
6. The gentle pastoral uplands district of the Lammermuirs is hardly the place where one would expect to find lions!
7. This saying has its origins in the large numbers of Scots soldiers that were drowned in the Till while retreating from Flodden Field where they were defeated by the English in 1513.
8. It is when the clouds are low that the rain will fall most heavily.
9. A saying referring to the most valued points of the four districts of the South West.

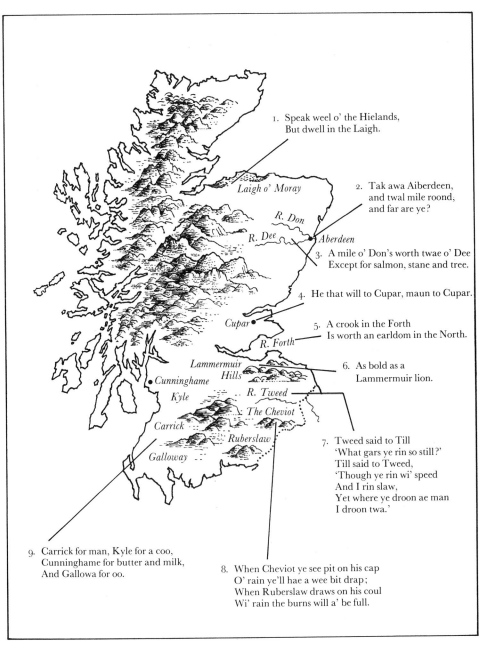

1. Speak weel o' the Hielands,
   But dwell in the Laigh.

*Laigh o' Moray*

*R. Don*

*R. Dee*

2. Tak awa Aiberdeen,
   and twal mile roond,
   and far are ye?

*Aberdeen*

3. A mile o' Don's worth twae o' Dee
   Except for salmon, stane and tree.

4. He that will to Cupar, maun to Cupar.

*Cupar*

5. A crook in the Forth
   Is worth an earldom in the North.

*R. Forth*

*Lammermuir Hills*

6. As bold as a
   Lammermuir lion.

*R. Tweed*

*Cunninghame*

*Kyle*

*The Cheviot*

*Carrick*

*Ruberslaw*

7. Tweed said to Till
   'What gars ye rin so still?'
   Till said to Tweed,
   'Though ye rin wi' speed
   And I rin slaw,
   Yet where ye droon ae man
   I droon twa.'

*Galloway*

9. Carrick for man, Kyle for a coo,
   Cunninghame for butter and milk,
   And Gallowa for oo.

8. When Cheviot ye see pit on his cap
   O' rain ye'll hae a wee bit drap;
   When Ruberslaw draws on his coul
   Wi' rain the burns will a' be full.

# PROVERBS

A proverb is a kind of saying which has a wise meaning. The words in a proverb make a picture of the meaning.

Many old Scots proverbs are hundreds of years old and have been handed down from generation to generation.

A – Abody ates a peck o' dirt afore they dee.
B – Better sit still than rise up and fa'.
C – Cheenges are lichtsome and fules are fond o' them.
D – Dincin aboot like a hen on a het girdle.
E – Every ane kens best where his ain shoe nips him.
F – Facts are chiels that winna ding.
G – Guid gear gangs intae sma bouk.
H – He that blaws in the stoor fills his ain een.
 I – If you dinna see the bottom, dinna wade.
 J – Jouk and let the jaw gae by.
K – Keep your gab steekit when ye kenna your company.
L – Lairn young, lairn fair; lairn auld, lairn sair.
M – Mickle spoken, part split.
N – Niver's a lang time.
O – Oot o' debt, oot o' danger.
 P – Put twa pennies in a purse and they'll creep thegither.
Q – Quick at meat, quick at work.
R – Royet lads mak sober men.
 S – Set a stoot hert tae a stey brae.
T – They craw crouse that craw last.
U – Unseen, unrued.
W – Wink at wee faults, your ain are muckle.
 Y – Ye canna mak a silk purse oot o' a soo's lug.

# *Mini-dictionary*
## OF SCOTS WORDS AND PHRASES

In this list you will find the meanings of some of the Scots words used in this book. Other words and expressions used by Scots children in their games and everyday life are also explained.

*a gane gyte*   all gone mad
*ablow*   below
*a'body*   everybody
*aboon, abune*   above
*aff*   off
*afore*   before
*ahent, ahint*   behind, after, at the
   back of
*aince*   once
*alane*   alone
*allo*   below
*ates*   eats
*atween*   between
*ava*   at all, of all
*ayont*   beyond

*ba'*   ball
*baggie*   bag
*bannock*   thick round cake of
   oatmeal
*bar*   to shut
*bawbee*   halfpenny
*bawk*   strip of untilled land
*beild*   shelter; image, figure
*besoms*   a term of contempt said to
   women
*birk*   birch
*birn*   load, crowd
*blether*   a bladder, chatter
*blooter*   smash
*bluid*   bold, blood
*bogle*   an apparition, ghost
*bool*   a boy's marble
*bouk*   to vomit

*bout*   a bolt
*braid-letter*   informal letter
*bree*   water in which any kind of
   food is boiled, gravy
*breist*   breast
*brent-new*   quite new
*brose*   oatmeal mixed with boiling
   water
*bubbly-jock*   turkey-cock
*buss*   bush

*cam*   came
*canny*   cautious, careful, shrewd
*cantraip-sleight*   conjuring trick
*cappie*   wooden cup or bowl
*carl*   old man
*carlin*   old woman, witch
*cauld*   cold
*caw the feet*   trip up
*cazy (cazzie)*   sack made of straw
*channerin*   grumbling
*chiel*   fellow
*chouks*   cheeks
*claes*   clothes
*claith*   cloth
*cleek*   a hook
*cleip*   to tell tales
*clert*   to soil, dirty
*cloot, clout*   a patch, rag
*cloot, clout*   to beat, cuff
*close-wa*   wall of passage
*clude*   a cloud
*coo*   a cow
*cooper*   a barrel maker

*coorse*  coarse
*coost*  cast out
*corbie*  crow
*cot-house*  farm worker's house
*cotillion*  type of dance
*coup*  tip up, overturn
*couples*  rafters
*cramasy*  crimson, crimson colour
*craps*  seed pods of runches or wild
    mustard
*craw*  to boast, brag
*creel*  a trap for catching lobsters
*crouse*  cosy, comfortable
*crouse*  cheerful, lively
*crousie*  merrily, briskly
*culdnae*  couldn't

*daen*  doing
*dauntit*  daunted
*daw*  dawn
*dee (deein)*  to die (dying)
*derk*  dark
*dincin*  dancing
*ding*  strike
*dinnle*  to rattle
*dirl*  resound
*dookin*  ducking
*doon*  down
*dout*  to doubt
*dreep*  drop
*dreich*  dull
*drookit*  drenched
*dune*  done
*dunnert*  stupid
*dyker*  a man who makes dykes,
    walls

*e'en*  eyes
*e'now*  just now, shortly
*efter*  after
*eldern*  elderly
*emerant*  emerald
*eneuch*  enough

*fa'*  to fall
*faem*  foam
*fail*  a flat sod of turf
*fail dyke*  wall built of fails
*fairin*  a drubbing
*fairins*  presents brought from a
    fair
*fash*  trouble
*fashes*  troubles
*faut*  fault, defect
*fecht*  to fight
*fee*  servant's wages
*feeing market*  hiring market for
    farm servants
*ferm*  farm
*fess*  to fetch
*flee*  to fly
*flichterin*  fluttering
*fly-cup*  a secret cup of tea, one
    taken on the sly
*forgethar*  to meet together
*forrit*  forward
*fou*  full, intoxicated, drunk
*freen*  friend
*freicht*  to frighten
*fules*  fools

*gab*  mouth
*gaed*  went
*gaislings*  goslings
*gait*  way
*gart*  made, compelled
*gear*  property, wealth
*gey*  very
*gibbet-airns*  irons, chains
*gin*  by the time that, if
*gird*  a child's hoop
*glaur*  mud
*gowd(en)*  gold(en)
*gowk*  cuckoo
*greetin*  crying
*grippit*  greedy
*guid*  good

*guise*   dress
*gundy*   candy, toffee

*hairst*   harvest
*hame*   home
*hantle*   large number
*hapt*   wrapped
*hauf*   half
*haun*   hand
*hause-bane*   neck-bone
*heckler*   flax dresser
*heeder*   header
*heeze*   to hoist
*heft*   a handle
*heich(est)*   high(est)
*hert*   heart
*hike*   to swing
*histie*   dry
*hither and yont*   hither and thither, backwards and forwards
*hiv*   to have
*hornies*   horns
*hummle their wulkies*   turn somersault
*hund*   a hound
*hunner*   a hundred
*hyow*   a hoe

*ile*   oil
*ilk*   each, every
*ill-trickit*   mischievous, roguish
*ither*   other

*jaud*   wild girl
*jaw*   a shower of rain
*jilp*   a spurt of water, liquid
*jine*   join
*jouk*   to take shelter from a storm

*kaims*   combs
*keekin*   peeping

*keepie-uppie*   a game in which a ball is kept in the air by head or foot
*kenna*   do not know
*kilt*   killed
*kintra-roon*   surrounding countryside
*kirn*   harvest home celebration
*kistie*   chest, box
*kype*   a hole in the ground used in playing marbles

*lairn*   learn
*lane*   alone
*lee (leein)*   to lie (lying)
*lichtsome*   cheerful, lively
*linn*   waterfall
*lippent*   expected
*loon*   boy, lad
*lug*   ear
*lum*   chimney

*maist*   most
*mak*   to make
*make a mane*   to complain
*mang*   amongst
*maun*   must
*mickle*   much
*mirk*   dark
*mirksome*   gloomy
*mony*   many
*moolie*   soft
*muckle*   great

*neebour*   neighbour
*neist*   next
*nicht*   night
*niver*   never
*nocht*   nought

*ony*   any
*oo*   wool

*oor* our, hour
*ower, owre* over

*pairtrick* partridge
*parritch* porridge
*pat* pot
*peerie* small
*pigger* an earthenware marble
*pike* to pick
*pit the hems* put paid to
*pith* substance, strength
*plooman* ploughman
*poke* bag
*preens* pins
*press* cupboard
*puir* poor

*rape* a rope
*raxin* stretching, straining
*reek* to smoke, smoke
*riven* worn
*rodden-tree* rowantree, mountain ash
*royet* mischievous, wild
*rype* to ransack, steal

*sair* sore
*sall* shall
*sapsy* cissy
*sark* shirt
*schule* school
*scurled* scabbed
*segs* sword shaped leaves
*share* cutting edge of plough
*shaughlin* shuffling
*Shelt* a Shetland pony
*sheugh* ditch, drain
*sic* such
*siller* silver, money
*simmer* summer
*sin* since
*skeely* skilful

*skirl* to scream, screech
*slee* sly
*sma'* small
*snowk(it)* to sniff(ed)
*sodger* soldier
*soo* sow
*sooms* swims
*stanie* stony
*steekit* shut tight
*steepies* milk and bread mixture
*stey* steep
*stick the heid* to butt
*stoot* stout, strong
*straucht* straight
*sybow* onion
*syke* marsh
*syne* since, ago

*tackety* hobnailed
*tak* take
*the gemmes a bogey* a cry to indicate that the game has been interrupted for some reason
*the tane* the one
*theek* to thatch
*thegither* together
*thon* 'yon', that
*tim* empty
*tod* a fox
*toon, toun* a town (*fermtoun* a farmstead)
*tow* flax, hemp
*tow-rock* flax distaff
*towzie* dishevelled
*twine* rope
*tyke* a rough, clownish fellow

*unco* every
*unhaily* unholy

*wald* would
*wale(d)* to pick(ed) out

wark(in) work(ing)
warlock a wizard
wasnae, wisnae wasn'
wean a child
wee small
weemen women
whaups curlews
whaur where
whiles sometimes
whilk which
wifie woman
wime the belly

winnock bunker window-seat
wot to know
wud wood


yestre' en last night
yett gate
yird earth
yoked started
yokin-time time to begin farm
    work
yont yonder, away

# Further Reading

The following may be of interest to those wishing to read further on the topics covered by the chapters in this book.

Aitken, Hannah (ed.), *A Forgotten Heritage*, Scottish Academic Press, 1973 (*Legends and Folklore*)

Annand, J. K., *Sing it aince for pleasure*, Macdonald, 1965, *Twice for joy*, MacDonald, 1973 (*Rhymes, Riddles*)

Buchan, D., *The Ballad and the Folk*, Routledge & Kegan Paul Ltd., 1972 (*Ballads and Folksongs*)

Buchan, N. (ed.), *101 Scottish Songs*, Collins, 1973 (*Ballads and Folksongs*)

Buchan, N. & P. Hall (eds), *The Scottish Folksinger*, Collins, 1973 (*Ballads and Folksongs*)

Budge, D. M. & G. Murray, *A Scottish Sampler*, Blackie, 1960 (*Proverbs and Sayings*)

Campbell, I. (ed.), *Come Listen*, Ginn, 1969 (*Ballads and Folksongs*)

Finlay, Winifred, *Folk Tales from Moor and Mountain*, Kaye & Ward, 1969 (*Legends and Folklore*)

Graves, R. (ed.), *English and Scottish Ballads*, Heinemann, 1967 (*Ballads and Folksongs*)

Jacobs, J. (ed.), *Celtic Fairy Tales*, Bodley Head, 1970 (*Legends and Folklore*)

Kinsley, J. (ed.), *The Oxford Book of Ballads*, Oxford University Press, 1969 (*Ballads and Folksongs*)

*The Lanimer Book of Verse*, Vols 2 & 3 (Revised editions) Blackie (*Mixter-Maxter*)

Leodhas, Sorche Nic, *Claymore and Kilt*, Bodley Head, 1971 (*Legends and Folklore*)

MacGillivray, A. & J. Rankin (eds), *The Ring of Words*, Oliver & Boyd, 1970 (*Mixter-Maxter*)

Macgregor, F., *Scots Proverbs and Rhymes*, Chambers, 1948 (*Proverbs and Sayings*)

MacMillan, A. (ed.), *The New Scots Reader*, Oliver & Boyd, 1972 (*Proverbs and Sayings*)

Montgomerie, N. &. W. (eds), *The Hogarth Book of Scottish Nursery Rhymes*, The Hogarth Press, 1964 (*Rhymes, Riddles*)

— *The Well at the World's End*, Bodley Head, 1975 (*Legends and Folklore*)

Opie, I. & P. (eds), *The Lore and Language of School Children*, Oxford University Press, 1959 (*Rhymes, Riddles*)

— *The Oxford Nursery Rhyme Book*, Oxford University Press, 1955 (*Rhymes, Riddles*)

Rintoul, D. & J. Skinner (eds), *Poets' Quair*, Oliver & Boyd, 1950 (*Mixter-Maxter*)

Ritchie, J. F., *The Singing Street,* Oliver & Boyd, 1964 (*Rhymes, Riddles*)

Scott, H. & T. (eds), *True Thomas the Rhymer and other tales of Lowland Scots,* Oxford University Press, 1971 (*Legends and Folklore*)

Scott, T. (ed.), *The Penguin Book of Scottish Verse,* Penguin, 1970 (*Mixter-Maxter*)

Wilson, Barbara Ker (ed.), *Scottish Folk Tales and Legends,* Oxford University Press, 1954 (*Legends and Folklore*)

Wood, Wendy, *Legends of the Borders,* Impulse Books, 1973 (*Legends and Folklore*)

Wyness, F., *Legends of North East Scotland,* Impulse Books, 1972 (*Legends and Folklore*)

A catalogue of Scottish Folksong Records can be obtained from: Topic Records, 27 Nassington Road, London, NW3 2TX.

## ACKNOWLEDGEMENTS

The editors and publishers are grateful to the following for permission to include copyright material:

Dr. W. R. Aitken and Benno Schotz for the photograph on page 15; J. K. Annand for the photograph on page 13, 'The Tod' (*Sing it Aince for Pleasure*) and 'Navy' (*Two Voices*); The Bodley Head for 'Jock and his Bagpipes' from *The Well at the World's End* by Norah and William Montgomerie; Patricia M. Black for the illustration on page 25; Ian Campbell for 'The Apprentice Song'; City of Edinburgh Museums for the illustration on page 46; Sheila Douglas for 'The Parking Song' and 'The Men o' the North'; *Dundee Courier* for the photograph on page 91; Edinburgh Public Library for the illustrations on pages 39 and 72; Faber and Faber Ltd. for 'The Fox's Skin' from *Turn of the Day* by Marion Angus; Glasgow Art Gallery for the illustration on page 25; David Higham Associates Ltd. for 'The Laird of Co' and 'My Own Self' from *Scottish Folk Tales* by Ruth Manning-Sanders; Hogarth Press and the authors for 'Unlucky Boat' from *Honour'd Shade* by George Mackay Brown and 'Interruption to a Journey' from *Surroundings* by Norman MacCaig and the photographs on pages 11 and 22; Lothian Studio for one cover illustration; Hugh McDiarmid for photograph on page 9, 'The Little White Rose' and 'The Bubblyjock'; Carl Macdougall for 'The Pretty Spotted Pig' and 'The Left-Handed Screwdriver' from *A Cuckoo's Nest*; Adam J. McNaughtan for 'The Jeely Piece Song'; Roberto Matassa for one cover illustration; Edwin Morgan for photograph on page 19 and, with Edinburgh University Press, 'The Chaffinch Map of Scotland' and 'The Computer's First Christmas Card'; Stephen Mulrine for photograph on page 24 and 'The Coming of the Wee Malkies'; National Gallery of Scotland for the illustration on page 26; Trustees of the National Library of Scotland and Dr. W. R. Aitken for 'Aince upon a Day' and 'Supper' by William Soutar; Thomas Nelson & Sons Ltd. for 'The Three Banshees' from *Scottish Legendary Tales* by Elizabeth Shepherd-Jones; Oxford University Press for 'The Barring of the Door' from *True Thomas the Rhymer and other Tales of the Lowland Scots* by Heather and Tom Scott (© Oxford University Press 1971); Phoenix Photos, Kirkwall for the photograph on page 56; the Scotsman Publications Ltd. for photographs on pages 50, 89 and 94; Scottish Academic Press and the author for 'Peerifool' and 'The Clever Apprentice' from *A Forgotten Heritage* by Hannah Aitken; Scottish National Portrait Gallery for the illustration on page 17; Scottish Tourist Board for three cover illustrations; Charles Skilton Ltd. for the excerpt from *Hard Shining Corn* by David Toulmin.

While every effort has been made to trace copyright owners, the publishers apologise for any omissions in the above list.

The editors would like to thank Mrs. Doreen Brown for typing the manuscript.